TOO DUMB FOR DEMOCRACY?

DAVID MOSCROP

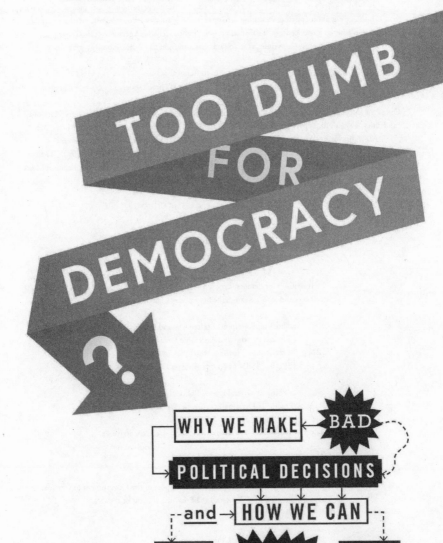

TOO DUMB FOR DEMOCRACY?

WHY WE MAKE BAD POLITICAL DECISIONS and HOW WE CAN make BETTER ONES

GOOSE LANE EDITIONS

Edited by Susan Renouf.
Cover design by Tree Abraham, Tree x Three Design.
Art direction and page design by Julie Scriver.
"Once in a Lifetime": Words and music by Brian Eno, David Byrne, Christopher Frantz, Jerry Harrison, and Tina Weymouth, copyright © 1980 by EG Music Ltd., WB Music Corp., and Index Music, Inc. All rights for EG Music Ltd., in the United States and Canada administered by Universal Music–MGB Songs. All rights for WB Music Corp., and Index Music, Inc., administered by WB Music Corp. International copyright secured. All rights reserved. Reprinted by permission of Hal Leonard LLC. Used by permission of Alfred Music.
Printed in Canada.
10 9 8 7 6 5 4 3 2 1

Library and Archives Canada Cataloguing in Publication

Moscrop, David, 1984-, author
Too dumb for democracy? : why we make bad political
decisions and how we can make better ones / David Moscrop.

Includes bibliographical references and index.
Issued in print and electronic formats.
ISBN 978-1-77310-041-8 (softcover).--ISBN 978-1-77310-042-5
(EPUB).--ISBN 978-1-77310-043-2 (Kindle)

1. Political psychology. 2. Political science.
3. Politics, Practical--Decision making. 4. Democracy. I. Title.

JA74.5.M67 2019   320.01'9   C2018-904592-2
                                            C2018-904593-0

Goose Lane Editions acknowledges the generous financial support of the Government of Canada, the Canada Council for the Arts, and the Province of New Brunswick.

Goose Lane Editions
500 Beaverbrook Court, Suite 330
Fredericton, New Brunswick
CANADA E3B 5X4
www.gooselane.com

For my dad, who isn't around to read this
but would have loved to brag about it to his friends;
and for my mom, who is around and who will do just that.

And to everyone who wants a shot at better democracy—
especially those for whom democracy has failed.
May this book be an arrow in their quiver.

Democracy is the theory that the common people know what they want, and deserve to get it good and hard.
—H.L. Mencken

Many forms of Government have been tried, and will be tried in this world of sin and woe. No one pretends that democracy is perfect or all-wise. Indeed, it has been said that democracy is the worst form of government except all those other forms that have been tried from time to time.
—Winston Churchill

If liberty and equality, as is thought by some, are chiefly to be found in democracy, they will be best attained when all persons alike share in the government to the utmost.
—Aristotle

We have forgotten that democracy must live as it thinks and think as it lives.
—Agnes Meyer

It's not the voting that's democracy, it's the counting.
—Tom Stoppard

Democracy begins with freedom from hunger, freedom from unemployment, freedom from fear, and freedom from hatred. To me, those are the real freedoms on the basis of which good human societies are based.
—Vandana Shiva

Contents

Preface

In the spring of 2008, I was sitting in a small room in a big house in Ottawa glancing back and forth between a studio piano that I had impulse-purchased a year before and never played and a shelf of books that had nothing to do with the project I was working on. I was completing my master's degree in political science at the University of Ottawa, writing my thesis on deliberative democracy—self-government based on dialogue and reason-giving. I needed a break, so I stood up and grabbed a book that looked interesting and that I could read for fun. I'd purchased it a few years earlier because it caught my eye and it was on sale.

Such is the role of remaindered books in history.

It was called *Looking for Spinoza: Joy, Sorrow, and the Feeling Brain* by neuroscientist Antonio Damasio. The title made me hopeful that somewhere in its 355 pages I might find some wisdom that would help me decide what to do with my life once I finished my degree: remain in Ottawa and go to work for a political party, start my PhD right away in Vancouver, or pack everything into storage and take off to South Korea to teach English. I was interested in all three options, but the latter two meant leaving a city I enjoyed and a woman I loved. Thinking about my future, I poured some coffee, opened the book, and sat down to explore the exciting and unfamiliar world of the human brain and mind—and to search for an answer to my young existential woes.

In the margins of that book, on page 8, I've drawn a vertical line and annotated it with a simple "Yes!" I rarely write in my books, so each time I do, I leave a reminder to myself that some passage must have struck me. In this case, I made it a measly eight pages before I discovered the lines, marked them, put the book down, and frantically called my supervisor, Paul Saurette. I can't recall for sure, but I doubt he'd said more than "Hey, Dave" before I interjected with, "I have to change *everything*!"

Damasio writes about why it is critical that insights from the natural and social sciences should underpin our understanding of decision-making. Reading him, I saw a career and a calling in front of me; it was a moment of revelation. Here are the lines that made such a difference:

> The success or failure of humanity depends in large
> measure on how the public and the institutions charged
> with the governance of public life incorporate that revised
> view of human beings in principles and policies. An
> understanding of the neurobiology of emotion and feelings
> is a key to the formulation of principles and policies
> capable of reducing human distress and enhancing human
> flourishing.[1]

Looking back, Damasio's point seems obvious, even self-evident. But it didn't seem that way to me that day. Instead, his argument was simultaneously a call to action and permission to think about scholarship and democratic life in broader, though still rigorous, ways.

A few minutes into my call with Paul, he had talked me down from a page-one rewrite of my thesis. He said something along the lines of, "Why not incorporate *some* neuroscience into your work and then return to it in your doctoral work?" I listened to his advice, thankfully, and wrote a thesis modelling how different approaches to democracy fit with insights from cognitive science. It was my first effort at trying to bridge understandings of human behaviour from the natural sciences with the political science of how we arrange societies and practise politics.

That effort lit a spark. When I boarded a plane to South Korea several months later to teach English in the charming-yet-bustling city of Suwon,

I did so with a plan to return to work on neuroscience and politics at the University of British Columbia.

Two years later, I started my PhD in the Department of Political Science at UBC. Over time, my obsession with neuroscience gave way to an interest in social and political psychology. My subsequent research into the psychology of deliberative democratic decision-making is the foundation of this book. The pages that follow are the product of my studies during the last decade, a stitching together of my attempts to understand how and why we live our political lives the way we do, and how we might live them in a more just, peaceful, inclusive, prosperous, rewarding, and stable way.

Introduction

And you may ask yourself
What is that beautiful house?
And you may ask yourself
Where does that highway go to?
And you may ask yourself
Am I right? Am I wrong?
And you may say to yourself
My God! What have I done?
　　　—Talking Heads

There was no way he was going to win. He was just running for the attention. He was in it for his own ego. He couldn't help it. He was there so that when he lost, he could start a cable news channel. All Trump, all the time: TNN, the Trump News Network.

Sure, America was heading towards a cliff. But they wouldn't throw themselves over the edge; eventually they'd stop. Before he won any primaries. Before he picked up steam. Before he became the nominee. Before he was elected president of the United States.

I was sitting on my couch with a friend when Donald J. Trump became the presumptive president-elect. Pizza. Beer. Shock. Disbelief. When it was clear that he had likely won, it was still early on the West Coast, where I was living. There it was. They'd done it. The unthinkable had not only become *thinkable* but *real*. As the final numbers rolled in, we turned off the television and the online feeds that had been giving us an IV drip of electoral returns, turned on my PlayStation 4, poured more beer, and played video games. Things were about to change. What's that line? Is it dancing in a thunderstorm? Or whistling past the graveyard?

The morning after Trump's win felt like the morning after you'd done something you were going to regret for a long time, except I'd done nothing but watch and worry. Immediately, I got calls from news outlets who wanted to talk about it. Why did it happen? How did it happen? Seriously, did that just happen? Could it happen elsewhere? Could it happen in the United Kingdom? Could it happen in France? Could it happen in, well, you know, could it happen in *Canada*? Aren't we better than that? And come to think of it, aren't Americans better than that?

History is always unfolding around us, but rarely do we think that it's happening while we're sitting on the couch or waking up in the morning, reaching for our phones to catch up on text messages, Facebook alerts, our Twitter stream, or the news. But every so often, something happens that feels *different*. Suddenly, history feels present. It feels heavy, like it's pressing on your chest with both hands. Trump's election was one of those moments.

So what do you do? After the election, my mind went to music. I listened to a lot of it. Just to think about something different. Before long, my shuffled tracks led me to Talking Heads — my favourite band. There came David Byrne's unmistakable voice and that pitch, that surprise, that feeling of incredulity-meets-alienation that he expresses in the song "Once in a Lifetime." Listening, I thought about Trump. And war. And nuclear weapons. And poverty. And climate change. In my head, I changed the song's *I* to *we* and asked, "What have we done?" And come to think of it, "Who are we exactly?"

Then it hit me: I know *exactly* who we are. I know *exactly* what we've done. We're a clever species that routinely makes bad decisions, including political decisions, and gets stuck living with the consequences.

With Trump's election, some humans made decisions poorly, and consequently the way we live together has been affected, mostly for the worse. Trump's election stands out, but it isn't the only example of such a phenomenon. In recent years, we have felt the weight of many bad political decisions. The United Kingdom held a messy referendum on leaving the European Union. The alt-right continued its climb in Europe and North America. Facebook, Twitter, and other digital platforms were widely used to manipulate political outcomes around the world. Climate scientists warned us that year after year was the warmest on record—and that temperatures were still climbing.

Not to be trite, but these things happen. We make bad decisions all the time. We all know that. But what's less often known is *why* we make bad decisions—and how we can make better ones. How did people end up with *these* political outcomes? And come to think of it, how do we make *any* sort of political decision, good or bad?

Now those are excellent questions. And I believe I have some answers. More importantly, I believe the answers to those questions are important. Very important. Our future depends upon good political decision-making. It depends upon us trusting our system, upon us seeing ourselves and our values and our desires reflected in it—all of us. And as a mix of old and new, even unprecedented, challenges threaten to upend democracy and even civilization, it is up to us to do better.

This book is about how we make political decisions, why we make bad ones, how we can make better ones, and why doing so is important. It is also about what better political decision-making means for the future of the United States, Canada, the United Kingdom, France, Germany, Australia, New Zealand, and dozens of other countries around the world that rely on their citizens to choose their governments and to express their opinions about what we ought to do together and how we ought to do it.

This book is also a yarn about you and me, about different countries, and about billions of people who find themselves sharing the planet at this very moment and who, I'm assuming, wish for future generations to share it, too. While the research and findings that I discuss may not apply to everyone everywhere, the argument I make applies to most people in most places who live, think, argue, opine, vote, and live their lives in diverse, complex, fast-paced countries marked by persistent differences of opinion and limited resources. Every day people are faced with important political decisions about what ought to be done, how, and why. Related to the question "What have we done?" is "How did we get here?"

To ask "How did we get here?" is to consider how we have evolved, how we have settled, how we have spread, how we have developed complex technologies and political institutions, and how we have decided — deliberately or otherwise — to live together on a planet that seems tiny when you consider the 7.6 billion of us who are here now.

Our evolution has unfolded over several million years, but our political institutions are of a much more recent vintage.[1] Permanent human settlements first popped up during the Neolithic Era, around 12,000 years ago. Civilization, as we understand it — in terms of more complex social systems of organization and communication — developed around 6,500 years ago. Recorded history entered the fray about 5,000 years ago. And the first democracy appeared in Ancient Greece about 2,500 years ago.

But our version of self-government, liberal democracy, is only about four hundred years old. It was birthed from ideas in the seventeenth century that led to the French Revolution and the American War of Independence, ideas including universal human rights, the rule of law, and government by elected representatives. But it didn't gain much traction until the nineteenth and twentieth centuries, when liberalism began to spread around the world and take the shape we recognize today.

So our democracy is of recent origin, and it's historically unusual. This development raises opportunities, but it also presents some challenges. The idea that all individuals have irrevocable rights and freedoms that not only include but also rely on self-government is revolutionary. Even Athenian democracy was limited to male, freeborn, native landholders. Additionally, the need, desire, and expectation that everyone should take part in political decision-making, both to protect rights and freedoms and to use them to decide how we are going to live together, is itself a remarkable achievement — one based on an ideal that we haven't fully realized.

As far as we've come, and as well as we're doing, we cannot sit back and congratulate ourselves. The future is not guaranteed, and we risk losing it all. There are injustices to overcome and institutions to protect. There are people on the outside who need in. To preserve ourselves, we must preserve democracy. To preserve democracy, we must make it just, inclusive, and participatory. We must learn to make good political decisions. That starts with fighting back against the many pressures, practices, and interests that work against our ability to do so.

Think about a country, any country, for a moment—the one you're living in, the one you were born in, the one you're visiting right now. What comes to mind? Perhaps it's geography: soaring mountains, rumbling oceans, expansive wheat fields, barren deserts. Or maybe you defaulted to social or cultural achievements: breathtaking works of art, stunning moments in sport, iconic buildings.

I'm Canadian. When I hear the word *Canada*, my automatic response is to think of the flag or Parliament Hill in Ottawa. It's not that I'm a fervent nationalist. Rather, as a student of political science, a writer who writes about politics, and someone who has lived off and on in my country's capital city, my national touchstones are political archetypes. My rapid default to the flag and the parliament buildings reminds me of cognitive linguist George Lakoff's book *Don't Think of an Elephant!* The joke, of course, is that upon hearing or reading the title, the first thing you think about is an elephant. You can't help yourself. Your mind goes where it is tipped to go.

Now, if you haven't already, think of the United States of America. I want to focus on it as a case study for a moment. For now, the United States is probably the most powerful country in the world, and as a diverse federation it is home to extremes that represent some of the best and worst of the political, social, cultural, and economic decisions and outcomes that we have achieved as a species. Both Abraham Lincoln and Donald Trump have served as president. The country was founded on a revolutionary idea of liberty but it accepted and defended slavery—and continues to suffer that legacy today. It is unimaginably wealthy, and yet millions live in poverty. It sent men to the moon but helped drive the world to the brink of climate disaster.

In 2018, the democracy watchdog organization Freedom House issued a report on freedom around the world, including a list of which countries were free or unfree.[3] In it, the United States earns a near-top ranking in freedom, civil liberties, and political rights with a total score of 86/100 (with a hundred being the "most free"). However, the report also raises concerns about the election of Donald Trump and the uncertainties for political liberty that come with his victory, especially considering Russian interference in American democracy. In a similar report, the Economist Intelligence Unit's *Democracy Index 2017*, showed the United States recently slipping, scoring a 7.98/10 and falling into the "flawed democracy" category (*prior* to Trump's election).[4]

Focusing on extremes, the United States spends $598 billion per year on defence while the next fourteen highest spenders combine for just a little more, $664 billion. Among the top countries on the index, America has an infant mortality rate of 6.1 deaths per one thousand live births, which puts it in last place of the twenty-eight wealthiest countries (for comparison, Finland's and Japan's rates are 2.3/1,000). The United States is second globally for its incarceration rate, after the Seychelles, with 666 prisoners per 100,000 persons. Americans also underperform in math and science. And life expectancy is lower than in its developed peers. Bad political decisions are undermining the country's potential—and its future. Where do these decisions come from?

Underlying decisions that affect infant mortality, education policy, life expectancy, and all the rest are *people*—not just elites such as politicians or academics, but everyone. Our choices create the environment in which we live. After all, in a democracy, it is we, the people, who are ultimately in charge. Sure, there are precedents, constraints, norms, and rules that shape our choices. But for a government to maintain trust and authority without resorting to violence or other forms of coercion, the people must accept that the laws and policies that are passed are at once just and legitimate. In other words, those laws and policies must have the broad support of those who make their preferences, values, and beliefs known to elected officials through elections or by sharing their opinions through letters and protests and polls. Developing and communicating those preferences is a process of political decision-making. And this political decision-making is essential to modern liberal democracy because the decisions of the government are supposed to reflect what the people want.

So the United States is doing well on some fronts and poorly on others. The same can be said of Canada and just about every other country in the world. You win some, and you lose some. You might be tempted to say that this is the same as it ever was, and there's not much we can do about it. Politicians are going to do what they are going to do. And besides, we have made so much progress. On balance everything is fine, right? Right?

Not so much. We find ourselves in a complex, frenetic, daunting world, one that is approaching a dangerous tipping point. Yes, we in the lucky democracies have more health, wealth, and safety than humans have ever had. Today, we have life expectancies into our seventies and eighties, mass interconnectedness, and the freedom to pursue the lives we wish to live in peace and security. And sure, as Harvard psychologist Steven Pinker has noted, violence is in long-term decline, and we may be living in the most peaceful time in history.[5]

But despite all the good we've managed to do, we have never faced the risks of mass casualty or extinction by our own hands that we face now. The invention and proliferation of nuclear weapons and the rise of human-caused climate change present existential challenges to our way of life and our existence. Overpopulation is also a threat, as is the rise of political extremism, global terrorism, and regional tensions around the globe. Pollution now kills an estimated *nine million* people a year.[6] Endemic poverty and preventable deaths are shameful embarrassments and massive problems, even though there is more global wealth than ever.

Creeping racism, sexism, and xenophobia have intersected with angry populism and authoritarianism, calling into question the future of liberalism and democracy. Democratic countries face challenges that include the marginalization and exploitation of certain populations, systematic discrimination, increasing wealth inequality, declining trust in politicians, and a lack of participation in self-government.[7]

Facing such serious threats, the impulse to retreat into cynicism or hopelessness, or to hope that someone else will look after our problems and abdicate our responsibility as citizens, is understandable. But we should not squander our future because things are tough. On the contrary, we should double down on democracy and get ourselves out of this mess. That process starts with knowing ourselves. The fact that we feel helpless or overwhelmed in the face of challenges that require us to make tough political decisions is not because we are terrible human beings but because we're imperfect and our abilities and resources are limited. And worse, our world is often an inhospitable place to make good political decisions. The news moves too fast. There is too much going on in our lives outside politics. We have too little time and energy to devote to learning about each and every thing that comes up. Issues are made more complicated and technical than they need to be. And some people make it their job to mislead or manipulate us. The political decision-making process is exhausting and discouraging, and it can make us feel like we are stuck on the outside with our faces pressed up to the glass.

The title of the book asks "Are we too dumb for democracy?" because we are often made to feel as if we are. But the answer is: *No, we're not too dumb for democracy*. We are, however, often stuck in situations that encourage or lead us to make dumb—or what I prefer to call bad—political decisions. It's not that we lack the capacity to make good political decisions but rather that we do not have the incentives, skills, resources, or opportunities to do so. And so we keep making bad political decisions. And they are catching up to us.

...

By now you are probably wondering, "Okay, so what's a bad political decision?" A bad political decision is one driven by bias, poor or incorrect information, or hidden motives. It is a decision that is often made on instinct, without research or reflection — the sort of decision we are likely to rationalize in the face of challenge or questioning. And it is something we're *all* prone to do, including me.

For instance, when I was younger, I joined the Liberal Party of Canada. I was a keener: I carried a membership card and everything. A leadership contest was underway, and the winner was going to become prime minister of Canada. I got involved to support a candidate who never ended up running, but I stayed on to support another contender. I was swept up in the moment: I'd been studying Canadian history and politics, I was fascinated with former Liberal prime minister Pierre Trudeau, and I was raring to go. I knocked on doors. I made phone calls. I signed up members. I raised money. I praised the party at every opportunity and defended it whenever it was necessary.

Now, there is nothing wrong with joining a political party or being excited about a candidate. But you should not switch off your brain as part of the process. Back then, if you had asked me why I was working on the leadership race, I would have given an answer about progress, about rights, about national identity, and about the future of the country. If you had pressed me for specifics or asked me about which policies of the candidates I supported and which I opposed, I would have drawn a blank — or, more likely, I would have tried to talk myself out of giving a specific answer. I was there because I was caught up in a moment; I was part of a team. And right up to the time I left the party, I wanted to win above all else, even if I was not willing to admit that to myself.

So what about good political decisions? My idea of a good political decision does not require any *specific* outcome. I do not presuppose that any opinion, policy, law, or electoral outcome is a good one simply because I agree with it, and I do not expect any outcome I disagree with to be a bad one. Sure, I have my own views, but in these pages, I mostly care about *process*. Why? Because the process of reaching a good decision is independent of political parties or affiliations. It doesn't matter if you're liberal or conservative. What matters is how you come to your conclusions and policies. And since democracy requires repeated political decisions over time, achieving and maintaining good processes, regardless of party affiliation, sets us up for success in the long run.

Now, it may be the case—I certainly think it is—that a bad decision-making process leads to bad outcomes. That is why I think Trump, Brexit, and climate change are the result of bad political decisions, both substantively and procedurally. It is why I think fixing the outcomes we get requires that we fix the process we use to make decisions.

So yes, process matters—a lot. Even if we agree that it is important that political decisions are fair, equal, and just and produce opinions, policies, laws, and electoral outcomes that allow us to live together peacefully, that is just the beginning. Since we often disagree with one another about what sorts of outcomes meet these standards (or even what these standards imply in the first place), the process by which we make decisions becomes the key to working out our differences, justifying our choices to one another, and bringing about a perception of trust and legitimacy in our democracy. After all, how often do we disagree with a political decision made by someone else? All the time. But we are more likely to accept that decision if we think it is the product of a process that we support as fair and legitimate. And even within ourselves, a good decision-making process can transform how we see the world, open us up to new perspectives, and help reinforce what we believe and why. So yes, getting to better decisions about what we ought to do requires that whatever else we do, we adopt a better process of decision-making.

You might think that in twenty-first-century democracies, we are already there. Throughout this book I will argue that we are not. For instance, however I feel about the substance of the Brexit referendum, the process was a mess in all kinds of ways. One of my favourite indicators of that is the fact that *after* the announcement that UK voters had elected to leave the European Union, the second most searched for question on

Google regarding the EU was "What is the EU?" And *just* ahead of the vote, one of the most common questions was "What is Brexit?" Yikes.

These searches imply that an alarming number of voters had no idea what they were voting for and no clue what they had done after they had cast their ballot. The day after Donald Trump was elected president offered similar results. That day, the top three "How did . . .?" questions on Google were "How did Trump win?" "How did this happen?" and "How did Clinton lose?" In this case, the searches might speak more to shock or curiosity than ignorance. But perhaps not.

During the election, Trump had run on a promise to repeal the Affordable Care Act, also known as Obamacare. After his win, many of his supporters expressed glee that the forty-fifth president was going to do away with Obamacare but were convinced that Trump would never dismantle the Affordable Care Act, with which they were becoming increasingly comfortable. That confusion was a long time coming. Years before Trump, in a 2013 CNBC poll, two similar groups were interviewed about health-care reform. One was asked about Obamacare, which 46 per cent opposed. The other group was asked about the Affordable Care Act, which 37 per cent of them were against. The two names referred to the same legislation.

In the Obamacare/Affordable Care Act instance, ignorance met framing. Bad political decisions are sensitive to the whims of a moment and to what psychologists call framing effects — the way an idea is presented. For instance, a proposed surgery might have a 90 per cent success rate or a 10 per cent failure rate. Despite the statistic implying the same risk, research reveals that patients responded more positively to the success percentage than to the failure rate.

In contrast to the shifting goalposts of a bad political decision, a good political decision is rational (informed, coherent, and consistent) and autonomous (the person knows why they made it and can explain their reasoning to you). We make good political decisions when we have enough good information to work with, the time and resources to sort through it, and the skills to work through what we want and why we want it. A good political decision also includes the ability to explain our reasoning to ourselves and to others. It's not enough to say *just because*, at least not if we want to meet the standards of a democracy in which we treat one another as citizens worthy of respect.

In short, a good political decision *belongs* to us. We make it ourselves, on purpose, and with full awareness of why we're making *that* decision and not *some other one*. You might think this is already how we make political decisions. We don't need research to tell us what a good or a bad decision is, we already know; and more to the point, we know that we happen to make *great decisions*. That is certainly how I used to think about things. But I was wrong.

So the short answer to "Are we too dumb for democracy?" is "Not really." The rest of this book is the long answer. It is the story of how we have found ourselves in a messy world where we must make important decisions. This is a world that we are often underprepared to navigate. It is a world where what we want and expect from ourselves is far greater than what we deliver. But that is just half the plot. The other bit of the tale I tell in these pages is the story of what our future can be if we choose to make good political decisions.

ONE

The citizen decision-maker

1. Public matters, grey matter:
The brain and decision-making

This book is full of reasons why we make bad political decisions, but none of those reasons are excuses for us to throw up our arms and say, "Well, what can you do? We are who we are." It is a bit too convenient to blame our bad political decision-making on our brains and then move on. What does that even mean? "My brain made me do it" is not a great defence. If you don't believe me, try using that line the next time you are pulled over for speeding. And yet understanding why we make bad political decisions — and why we end up with regrettable outcomes — requires that we first understand the brain and how it works.

Let's begin with the idea that we *Homo sapiens* are more than just a brain. Because of course we are. But we are also nothing without it. The brain is essential to human life, not just to keep our bodies working — without the autonomic nervous system to regulate blood flow, breathing, hormones, and so forth, we would not last long — but also to make consciousness possible. Through a process that continues to elude researchers, the brain, the body, and the outside world interact to produce self-awareness and subjectivity — that experience of the world that makes us who we are.

The brain also does all kinds of other useful things. It allows us to make and recall memories. It serves as a central processing centre so that you can take in and move throughout the world. It makes speech possible. Most importantly, the brain not only enables thinking but allows us to *think about thinking*. This quality makes it possible for us to make decisions and then *to reflect on them*: why we made them, whether they were good or bad, and how they might be improved in the future. So to understand how and why we make the political decisions we do, we must start with a tour of our brains.

Picture a brain. Pinkish, shaped like a football that is flattened out on the bottom, separated into two hemispheres, and marked by a distinctive pattern of folds. That is the outer layer of the brain, the cerebral cortex, and it is further divided into regions. One of those regions is the neocortex and it makes up most of the cerebral cortex's area. This part is sometimes referred to as the thinking brain. It is what allows us to engage in behaviours that we think of as distinctively human—having a conversation, singing a song, solving a complex math equation, writing a book, performing surgery, mastering a video game.

The evolution of the neocortex is the result of a long process of natural selection that has also made us good at problem solving. In *How to Create a Mind*—a book about developing artificial intelligence by reverse engineering the brain—scientist and futurist Ray Kurzweil asks, "If the neocortex is so good at solving problems, then what is the main problem we are trying to solve? The problem that evolution has always tried to solve is survival of the species. That translates into the survival of the individual, and each of us uses his or her own neocortex to interpret that in myriad ways."[1]

That sounds about right. However, if our main driver is survival, we are currently putting a lot of what seems like unnecessary pressure on our individual and collective brains as our clever ability to create new things continues to outpace our ability to responsibly control the tools and technologies we come up with. (Think of nuclear weapons or, well, social media.)

At the same time, the fact that our brains are geared towards ensuring survival may in fact explain our fascination with (potential) mass catastrophes. Just think of the books we write, the films we watch, the songs we sing, the technologies we develop, and a whole host of other social, cultural, and scientific activity. We crave disaster, and that may be because disaster is a good teacher. It turns out that we learn more from negative examples than positive ones, a tendency that social scientists call our "negativity bias." If one of our savannah-roving forebears ate something poisonous, it alerted his fellows to stay away from that food and to survive to search another day. That was good news for our forebears who struggled to survive hand to mouth in treacherous locales; it is less good news today when exploited by political actors with sophisticated techniques who are looking to manipulate you into voting — or not voting — one way or another, or when the negative examples we produce could destroy civilization.

We also crave survival. Next time you are in a bookstore or scrolling through Netflix offerings, pay attention to the wide selection of End Times fare: gigantic meteors striking Earth, alien invasions, pandemics, earthquakes, floods, drought, nuclear war, and, of course, mass zombification. They all portray destruction but also humanity's innate desire to remain alive. This drive does not just apply to those of us who are here now. It shows our ambition to procreate and pass on our genes to the next generation. Presumably, that includes leaving our children a habitable planet. Our determination to survive exceeds and goes beyond our immediate existence; we project it forward in time and shape our lives with it in mind.

Our intergenerational commitment to survival is part of the reason why potential catastrophes like those that will come from climate change run amok are so serious, and another reason why good political decision-making is so important. We want to stick around, and we need to figure out how to do that. I'm betting the farm — and everything else — on the idea that we can maximize our chances of survival by adopting a good process for making political decisions. That said, we are up against a long history of pushing our luck, of driving ourselves to the edge of destruction.

...

Precedents for climate-based disaster caused by humankind stretch back *thousands of years*. That's right: we're making mistakes like those made by our Bronze Age predecessors. In Ancient Mesopotamia, residents farmed their rich fields until so much salt accumulated in them that it became impossible to grow enough food to sustain the population.[2] The decline of Ancient Mesopotamia was precipitous and disastrous. It was also early proof that as impressive as the neocortex is, humankind often faces challenges that we are unprepared, unwilling, or unable to overcome.

A few thousand years after that, in the fifth century CE, Rapa Nui (also known as Easter Island) was settled. In his 2004 Massey Lecture and book *A Short History of Progress*, Ronald Wright discusses the rise and fall of the people who lived and died on the 164-square-kilometre island. There, local clans engaged in competitive ancestor worship by building stone statues, which required considerable resources. As Wright tells us:

> Each generation of images grew bigger than the last, demanding more timber, rope, and manpower for hauling to the ahu, or altars. Trees were cut faster than they could grow, a problem worsened by the settlers' rats, who ate the seeds and saplings. By AD 1400, no more tree pollen is found in the annual layers of the crater lakes: the woods had been utterly destroyed by both the largest and the smallest mammal on the island.... Wars broke out over ancient planks and worm-eaten bits of jetsam. They ate all their dogs and nearly all the nesting birds.... There was nothing left but the moai, the stone giants who had devoured the land.[3]

You might think the inhabitants of Mesopotamian city states should be forgiven for their ignorance of salinization, but evidence suggests they knew what they were doing. The same is true for Rapa Nui's dwellers. They could count the trees remaining as they felled them, one by one.

They put their hope in an expected mystical salvation and rationalized their consumption by their need to worship in the same way they had always worshipped in search of salvation.

But before we indulge our impulse to judge the long-vanished residents of Ancient Mesopotamia or Rapa Nui, we should look at ourselves first. Like the Mesopotamians, we have destroyed plenty of land. And as for the folks who inhabited Rapa Nui, if you swap *mystical* for *technological* and *worship* for *consume*, you'll quickly find some disconcerting similarities between them and us.

Like humans today, the lives of those who lived on Rapa Nui were marked by a tension between necessity and desire — or between survival and the social, political, economic, and cultural practices of the day, some of which were part of the drive to survive, some of which were not, and some of which were mistakenly thought to be. We do not need all that much to survive, especially compared to all the stuff we have access to. But we've come to expect that it takes a lot to survive, and even more to be content, although abundance rarely does the trick.

Therein lies the trap. Our advancements have made life more predictable and stable than ever before, but they have led to new and serious problems that we are hesitant to tackle.

But why? If our brains have evolved to, among other things, solve problems and help us survive as a species, how do we end up in such debilitating existential conundrums? Well, the answer starts with an explanation of what the brain is and, importantly, what it is not.

When speaking about the brain we often reach for a computational metaphor: the brain as a computer. But our brain is not a computer, and we certainly do not think in the same way a computer "thinks." When I turn on my computer in the morning and open my email, my brain often stops me, a voice creeping in to say, "Are you *sure* you want to do this? Maybe fifteen more minutes of video games first." But my computer does not try to stop me, as much as I might wish it would; it just does what it is instructed to do. Computers accept inputs and produce predictable outputs. They do not editorialize. They do not jump to conclusions. They do not battle internally over whether they ought to open a word processor or drink another coffee on the patio. They are not driven by emotion or hidden motivations. They are machines that are insensitive to the environment in which they operate. We are quite the opposite.

Gerald Edelman, a Nobel Prize-winning biologist who spent the later part of his career studying the nature of human consciousness, described the differences between computer thinking and the thinking we do as humans. The brain does not function by logical rules, argued Edelman.[4] While a computer uses logic as a *rule*, we do not. Computers are consistent; we are not. Computers are identical; no two brains are the same. Computers are assembled and programmed to be fixed—that is, to respond the same way based on specific commands. Brains are constantly in flux based on new and changing information from the environment in which they exist. The brain has not evolved for knowledge, and it certainly was not deliberately designed for it. Rather, it has evolved to undertake a complex, sometimes paradoxical, suite of functions that are often complementary but sometimes trip one another up.

If the brain is not a computer, what is it? Well, for one thing, it is an organ, but not just any organ. The brain is the primary site of the human central nervous system. It directs traffic, both internally and externally, receiving sensory signals from outside the body and sending others through the body.

Recall that we are the product of millions of years of evolution. In his sweeping history of humankind, *Sapiens*, historian Yuval Noah Harari notes that for a long time, we did not accomplish much in terms of applying our comparatively large brains. As he puts it, "For more than 2 million years, human neural networks kept growing and growing, but apart from some flint knives and pointy sticks, humans had precious little to show for it."[5] Then, during the Cognitive Revolution about seventy thousand years ago, things changed. Humans started to explore, to invent, and to make art. Suddenly, our ancestors found new ways to think and to communicate with one another. The rate of change sped up. We used increasingly sophisticated tools and weapons; we domesticated animals; we took up agriculture; and we dispersed across the world. We developed writing systems and languages; we made art and eventually wrote down some of our stories. We gathered into urban areas and needed systems by which we could govern ourselves. We found ourselves a species with organized politics. We created democracy. We built nuclear weapons. We went to the moon. We brought on climate change. We invented fidget spinners.

The legacy of these advances in language, art, engineering, architecture, law, and dozens of areas of human accomplishment is embedded in our brains. Wherever we go, wherever we are, we carry with us the story of millions of years of development. Today that legacy often presents itself as a tension between what we are asked and expected to do and our pre-wired inclinations and responses.

What is that tension about? One way to think of the human brain is to divide it into rational and emotional modes. Another is to divide it into conscious and unconscious modes. But in doing this, we are oversimplifying and reducing our immensely complex brain architecture to ideal types based on how the brain functions and in what sort of state it does the functioning. There is something useful in this practice, so I am going to adopt these simplified types to help us understand the organ from which our decision-making springs. But keep in mind that the brain is not this tidy. It is a constant whirling mix of rationality and emotion, of conscious and unconscious processing. That said, for our purposes, let's pretend for a minute that it is simpler than that and meet our brain types.

The emotional brain and the rational brain

The first set of brains we will meet are the emotional brain and the rational brain. Let's start with the emotional one. The limbic system is buried deep in our brain, where it comprises a few areas including the hippocampus, the amygdala, and the hypothalamus. The areas of the limbic system are related to autonomic regulation (think of your heart and respiratory rates, digestion — all the essential things your body does without you having to think about it) and emotion. This region is also linked to hunger, thirst, body temperature regulation, sexual desire, fear, empathy, and threat recognition. The limbic system is found deep in the brain structure because it is old — very old. The evolution of the brain has been a process of layering new bits overtop old ones, and this region is on the bottom. The areas of the limbic system are primarily associated with functions that emerged early on in our development as a species. These are the ancient bits.

This region is often thought of as the emotional brain because it captures the part of us that is bound up in the early days of our evolution, with those automatic, often-instantaneous emotional reactions to the world. It is also in this part of our brain that the famous "fight or flight" response resides.

Psychologist and psychiatrist Drew Westen calls this type "the passionate brain" instead of the emotional brain. But it is the same idea. He highlights that emotions serve a key function in human behaviour: they help us survive.

Each of us can think of an instance in our lives in which the passionate brain took charge, for better or worse. Nearly a decade ago, I was travelling with a friend, Kristin, in Toulouse, France, the stunning Ville Rose (Pink City), the capital of the country's southern Occitanie region. We were settled along the Canal du Midi, which links the city to the Mediterranean Sea. There we sat, enjoying a drink, chatting idly, plunked down on a bench beside the water. After a while, two men walking towards us started to drift closer and closer to where we were sitting. Suddenly, one man deliberately stumbled into us and grabbed my camera, which Kristin was holding. She and I both shot up. I clenched my fists and moved towards them, but not before Kristin had done the same, screaming at them and threatening to take the camera back — and then some. Her limbic system had quickly processed the fight or flight options and chosen the former.

After a moment, I noticed something in the hands of one of the muggers. It was a bottle of pepper spray, pointed towards our faces. Kristin thought it was a lighter and kept up the fight. I nudged her and whispered, "Pepper spray." She looked down at the canister and back at me. The men backed away, my camera in hand.

As they left, Kristin, her rational brain outpacing my own by miles, called after them in flawless French, "Our vacation pictures are on that memory card. Give it back." The men stopped a few metres away and turned back towards us, replying in French, "Okay, just shut your mouths, and stay put." They removed the memory card from the camera, tossed it onto the ground, and walked away into the night.

My experience in Toulouse is a reminder that sometimes the emotional or passionate brain, which has evolved to help us survive, requires moderation even as it remains an integral part of the human experience. Both Kristin and I wanted to choose fight over flight, and we almost did. But that would have been a disaster. The ideal of the rational brain stands in stark contrast to the passion of the emotional brain. I say *ideal* because the rational brain model is often held up as an example of how we *should* think, although research suggests that purely rational thinking, without emotional intervention, would be closer to sociopathy than the Enlightenment model of the rational and reflective individual.[6]

The rational brain is dispassionate. Compared to the passionate emotional brain, it is cool, calm, slow, and measured. It is where we think. Anatomically, it is associated with the cerebral cortex, that outer layer on top of the cerebrum we talked about earlier. Evolutionarily speaking, this bit of the brain developed more recently than our limbic brain and, in humans, is much larger as a percentage of total brain size than in other mammals.

The rational brain allows us to consider that the best way to make a choice is by collecting information, reflecting on it, weighing the pros and cons and implications of our options, discussing and debating the matter with others, and then coming to a decision about what ought to be done and why. Versions of how we have used our rational capacity in this way in the West are recorded as far back as Plato, over 2,400 years ago. More recently, Enlightenment philosophers seized and developed this approach, and revolutionaries who tried to engineer new societies from the ground up in the eighteenth and nineteenth centuries put it into practice.

These thinkers and doers upset hundreds of years of tradition and practice in search of a new foundation for social and political order in Europe and America. And in doing so, they gave rise to new ideas and practices of rights and freedoms that we hold dear today. But they also indulged in bloody revolutionary excesses and triggered conservative backlashes. So our rational brain, like our emotional brain, is far from infallible. We expect more from ourselves than we can deliver with our grandiose ideas about our rationality, which can get us into trouble, as mine and Kristin's almost did that night in Toulouse.

That said, our emotional brain tends to do most of the heavy lifting when it comes to making bad political decisions. Of course, it does it from a place of love. Kind of. As Westen puts it, "Emotions channel behavior in directions that maximize our survival, reproduction, and care for the welfare of others in whom we are emotionally invested."[7] That's nice. But here we encounter the problem with the emotional or passionate brain: while it has evolved to help us survive, it is also subject to bias, especially towards those we think of as our "ingroup" and with whom we have an emotional connection.

The term *ingroup* refers to a concept used in psychology, sociology, and political science to refer to a social group to which a person belongs — or at least *identifies* as belonging to. Membership in an ingroup can develop over a short or a long period, and it can be based on something trivial, such as hair colour (put your hand up if you, like me, are a ginger), or something more substantive, such as family, ethnicity, class, or religion.

In politics, one sort of ingroup is the political party you support or belong to. This is known as partisanship, and in one way or another it has been an important part of politics for hundreds of years. We might think of partisan politics as rational and policy based, but that is usually a stretch.

Years ago, my grandfather told me a story he had heard — perhaps apocryphal — about two brothers who lived in Newfoundland. One was a

Liberal and one was a Conservative. Each was deeply wedded to his party and despised the other one. They ran a family business together, which was tough since they spent their days fighting about politics. One day they decided that the only way the business would survive is if they shared custody of it: when the Liberals were in power, one brother would remain on the island and run the show; when the Conservatives were in power, the other would swap in for him. The two were so affected by partisanship that it controlled their professional and personal lives.

Partisanship, as an emotional-brain response, tends to shape how we think as much as it reflects our thinking. When we consider political loyalties, we might think we choose our party based on what we believe, but it is often just the opposite. When the emotional brain becomes attached to an identity — like partisanship — it tends to shut out, or at least attenuate, the rational brain. In doing so, it shapes our perception of the world in ways that facilitate keeping that emotional connection and protecting our ingroup. When this happens, we get stereotyping and chauvinism instead of calm, dispassionate calculation. So, it should come as no surprise that when looking at a political leader, partisans often fit their evaluation of that person to preconceived notions about what a Liberal, Conservative, Democrat, or Republican *should* be rather than bothering to learn who that person actually is.

In *Partisan Hearts and Minds*, political scientist Donald Green and his colleagues argue that partisanship in America is often learned at a young age.[8] Once learned, partisans identify with their ingroup and develop a strong desire to see themselves (and their party) as good. To do so, they shape their worldview (and ignore or manipulate facts) to preserve both their partisan identity and the belief that their team is the good team. That is the emotional brain at work.

I bet you have met someone like this. "That guy is *really* a Liberal," you thought, or, "That woman is *such* a Republican." The next time you are out in the world or using social media, keep your eye out for partisans. They can often be spotted by the conspicuous rationalizations or confabulations they use to defend their point of view. Some of them are so clouded by their partisan commitment that they can be difficult to persuade or learn from — or even talk to. You can try, of course, but that way madness lies.

Lots of great research on partisan identity comes from the United States. No surprise. There are plenty of high-profile examples from south of the border that illustrate how partisanship is one hell of a drug. But lest we think that this phenomenon is just some American peculiarity, consider an example from Canada in the early 2000s. During those years, the Liberal Party was in hot water over something known as the sponsorship scandal. A kerfuffle that would eventually cost the Liberals their government majority — and, later, the government all together — the affair involved the misuse of public money meant to fund federal government advertising in Quebec. Millions of dollars were spent for very little work and considerable sums of money went to Liberal-friendly advertising firms. When political scientist André Blais and his colleagues studied the reaction of Canadians outside of Quebec to the scandal, they found that Liberal partisans were less likely than others to believe that Paul Martin, then finance minister and a Quebec member of Parliament himself, had known about the shady dealings.[9] If you listen carefully, you can hear, "*Sure*, politicians are shady. But not *our guy*."

As much as we might prefer to think of ourselves as calculating machines governed by our rational brain, the truth is that our emotional brain is frequently at the helm. So the fact that we are often of "two brains" complicates our understanding of ourselves and our behaviour. But things are even messier than that. Not only are we divided between a rational and an emotional brain, all jumbled together in real time, but we can further divide the brain into two more types.

The conscious brain and the unconscious brain

Despite how impressive our brains are, much of our "being human" happens without us even noticing. That might seem strange to you. Consciousness enjoys pride of place in our sense of self (even if it is not unique to our species). The headline stuff of human experience is based on consciousness: the awareness that we exist, that others exist, and that there is a world outside of ourselves in which existence is playing out. However, most of what we take in around us is not consciously registered. Neuroscientist Michael Gazzaniga estimates that as much as 98 per cent of activity in the brain is *unconscious*.[10] While this unregistered activity includes basic survival functions like digestion and body temperature regulation, it also includes receiving and processing stimuli from the outside world that are taken in by other regions of the brain.

A lot is going on inside our heads that we do not have access to, but it affects us nonetheless: our mood, our goals, our behaviour, and our decisions. In a now famous experiment by researchers Christopher Chabris and Daniel Simons, subjects were asked to watch a video in which six people, half wearing white shirts and half wearing black shirts, pass a basketball back and forth. The subjects were tasked with keeping a count of how many passes the folks in white made. During the video, a gorilla (that is, a person in a gorilla suit) walks into the frame, thumps its chest, and walks off—after spending a total of *nine seconds* on screen. Remarkably, *half of those* who watched the video and kept count of the passes failed to register the gorilla: half (including me). So whatever you might think about how you perceive and register the world, the truth is that you cannot help but miss an awful lot, at least consciously.[11]

The competitive companion of the unconscious brain is the conscious brain: the one that recognizes what is going on around us, the one that focuses on the task at hand, the one we use to reason. The conscious brain is a more recent development in our evolutionary history. When we try to explain why we are for or against free trade or attempt to track closely what political leaders say in a debate, we are engaging our conscious brains. But this is the brain we know, the one we think about when we think about brains. It is the one reading these words, the one telling you that once you finish this chapter, you can have a snack.

Unconscious information processing happens all the time, and it plays an important role in our day-to-day lives. From an evolutionary standpoint, this makes a lot of sense. Imagine having to register and think about everything that goes on around and inside you at every minute of the day: all the sights, the sounds, the smells. All the internal processes necessary to keep you alive: your heartbeat, breathing, body temperature. Everything. You would never get anything done. More importantly, you would be miserable. Your limited attention resources would be overwhelmed, and your ability to react quickly would be smothered. You wouldn't survive long. Imagine suddenly coming across a predator in the wild. To take the time to deliberate over whether to flee would give that predator just enough time to turn you into a meal. Or imagine entering a crosswalk just as a car does: the split second in which you stop or leap backwards or the driver hits the brakes could be the difference between life and death.

But your unconscious brain does not just regulate internal function and tell you when to leap to safety. It processes day-to-day stimuli that affect your conscious behaviour and judgment, for better and for worse, outside of your awareness. This is where we get into trouble, especially these days. The phenomenon of automaticity is an example of this. One form of automaticity is acquired, like when you have learned to play the guitar or catch a ball. You just do it. If you slow down to think about what you're doing, the activity often becomes more difficult. Not only is this form of automaticity mostly harmless, but it is usually a major asset and the result of long periods of deliberate, focused practice. You first pick up your guitar and slowly place your fingers to fret a note or a chord. You press down and pluck the string only to hear a muted *twang*. You then lift your fingers and think about the next note or chord, moving them one by one, placing them in just the right spot. And then, again, a dull *twang*. Within a few days of practice, your movement picks up, and the sounds you are making become less muffled. Within a few weeks, you can hear a song. Months later, you are moving from note to note and chord to chord without even thinking about it. Before long, they will be filling stadiums with people eager to hear you play.

But there is another form of automaticity, one where stimuli affect your behaviour not deliberately but *outside* of your awareness. In this case, the brain generates outputs like moods or judgments without also generating a conscious awareness of *why* we are making that judgment or feeling that way. It happens all the time. If you have ever felt just a bit, well, off or suddenly angry or uncomfortable but did not know why, you have experienced automaticity at work. It is likely that your brain picked up on something you didn't consciously notice and cued the appropriate feeling-state. From there on, it is hard not to let those feelings affect what you are doing.

Most of us have woken up one morning feeling strange, perhaps even angry at someone in our lives without knowing why. Most of us have also experienced a midday shift in our mood, seemingly out of nowhere. Think back. You're sitting at your desk or walking along and the world is your oyster. Half an hour later, you're on a rampage: frustrated, irritated, sour. That comes from somewhere, even if you're not sure where. Did someone say something? Did you catch something out of the corner of your eye? Did a song come on that triggered a bad memory?

When it comes to politics, the unconscious brain can contribute to poor decision-making by initiating responses to the world outside of your awareness. For instance, implicit biases, such as racism, can easily creep in to political decision-making, affecting how we feel about issues or candidates. In those instances, when we are later asked to explain ourselves, to give an account of why we are for or against some proposition, or why we support this candidate or that one, we often find ourselves at a loss. Or we might simply make something up and try to rationalize our way to a conclusion.

There are plenty of examples of implicit bias in politics, but I want to start with sports, which is home to all kinds of wacky ways of thinking.

Nearly every single one of us who has a favourite sports team, if we're being honest with ourselves, knows this to be true.

I'm a big fan of the Detroit Red Wings. I have been since I started watching hockey as a kid. I don't have many chances to watch them play these days, and I'm not able to name the roster like I could a decade ago, but when I do catch a game, I find myself not just pulling for them, but cursing the referees for the *terrible* calls they make against the team compared to their opponents. Why is it that every call against my team is a bad one? Why is it that every call against the opposing team is a good one? Could it be that every referee in the history of sport is in the bag for the team competing against my favourite squad? It must be.

Sports is a haven for implicit bias, and so is politics, which is often treated like a sport. In a telling study that I will return to later, researchers Charles Ballew and Alexander Todorov found that citizens made rapid judgments of "competence" based on one hundred milliseconds of exposure to the faces of candidates in an American gubernatorial election.[12] These rapid judgments predicted who was going to win the race. In some cases, in fact, longer exposure to photos of the candidates *reduced* predictability. Sometimes we simply, immediately think we know something—like what it means to look competent. It may be neither accurate nor useful. But we know. We just know.

Our brains evolved with the twin abilities for both focused and non-conscious processing. These abilities have allowed us to zero in on tasks while also remaining "aware" of our surroundings. However, since the brain in action is a complex, messy series of interactions, these two abilities or tracks of thinking overlap. That means that when we make political decisions, we're often drawing on both conscious and non-conscious influences—sometimes for better, often for worse.

When it comes to understanding the brain and behaviour, there is a real and constant struggle between our preferences, goals, expectations, needs, and biological drives. It is our capacity to make decisions that helps us adjudicate these different considerations, which are often competing with one another—especially when it comes to making short-, medium-, and long-term plans.

Take an example that I bet you will find familiar. Each morning when your alarm goes off, you have a few options. You can hit the snooze button (or swipe across the screen, if you use your phone as an alarm, like I do). You can hurl the clock, phone, or whatever you use, across the room and decide that today is an in-bed day. You can seize the moment: put both feet on the ground, get up, shower, grab some breakfast, and get to work. Each of these choices has consequences. Hitting the snooze button gives you longer to rest but leaves you with less time to get to work or get things done. Getting up increases how much time you have to accomplish tasks and enjoy the company of others, but it may leave you less rested than you would like to be. Throwing your alarm clock across the room may give you a pleasant day in bed with some television and take-out, or a deep, almost transcendent, sense of satisfaction, but you'll also have to buy a new alarm (or phone), and you may have to explain why you were not at work or school.

This example is frivolous, of course, but it highlights a problem we face when trying to understand how brain and behaviour relate to one another and to notions of self, self-determination, and freedom. When our alarm rings, who are we? And who is in charge? The me who set the alarm the night before? The me who's about to act? The me who propels my expensive smartphone across the room and into oblivion? Moreover, what is driving my action? Am I *really* thinking about what I am doing? After all, how many times have you woken up late only to ask yourself: how did I end up sleeping in *again*? How did I end up hitting the snooze button three times *again*? I don't even remember doing that! Who's running this show, anyway?

Let's take the spirit of this example and get back to politics and how our brains shape and constrain our political behaviour. In *Political Animals,* journalist and historian Rick Shenkman argues that our brain evolved for the Pleistocene Era—a geological epoch that stretched from about 2.6 million years ago to about 12,000 years ago—and so it is not well adapted for Information Age politics.[13] As a species, we evolved tendencies and instincts over millions of years that were well adapted to a much simpler, slower world. Today, our brains often just cannot keep up. We are asked to follow the news, scrutinize complex policy proposals, adjudicate between competing arguments, track the promises and records of politicians, and turn up to town halls, public debates, and election days. Yet for most of us, these things are of secondary concern to our immediate day-to-day obligations: working, raising our families, and enjoying the little free time we have. As Shenkman points out, this does not mean that we are destined to fail in our democratic endeavours. But it does mean that we face a challenge, as our deep-rooted tendencies and instincts come up against modern ways of living that can be inhospitable to them. Our cognitive evolution has not been able to keep up with our social, political, cultural, and technological evolution.

We have met our four brains, so we can now ask how, exactly, does the brain as a whole work when it comes to making political decisions? Let's get into this by imaging two highly stylized decision makers: Claudia from New York and Andrew from Vancouver.

Claudia represents the classic Enlightenment decision-maker: dispassionate, autonomous, rational. Before she decides, she collects evidence, weighs the pros and cons of her different options by comparing that evidence, and thinks about the short-, medium-, and long-term opportunity costs. She considers the most efficient way to maximize specific, pre-determined goals for herself. For the most part, she shuts out her emotions and focuses on rationally considering the matter at hand. When you ask her to decide, she fires off reasons for and against, she cites evidence, and, well, she just looks like she knows what she is doing. Evolutionarily speaking, she engages the newer bits of her brain, those associated with the recently evolved cerebral cortex. While Claudia is a caricature, she represents a classical rationalist model of cognition associated with the cerebral cortex's frontal lobes, which are found just behind your forehead. I imagine Claudia making a decision, staring out the window of one of the gargantuan glass office buildings you find on Wall Street, hands intertwined behind her back, chin up, eyes focused on the horizon, the cogs in her head turning steady and deliberately.

Now imagine Andrew from Vancouver. His decisions are less rational than Claudia's. Indeed, he is the consummate emotional decision maker. He relies on his gut, on his feelings, and tends to make rapid, snap judgments that influence his decisions. He has deep emotional commitments that drive his reasoning process, and he relies on shortcuts—which are prone to bias—to help him navigate complex decision-making territory. When you ask him to decide, he looks at you and says, "Well, I don't know, but my gut says I should do this. I don't know why I know, I just know." While Andrew's approach to decision-making also involves the brain's frontal lobes, it draws heavily on the older bits of the brain. I imagine Andrew making a decision while enjoying a day out at one of Vancouver's many sandy beaches—staring out, perhaps, at English Bay and looking across at the North Shore mountains—and then quickly darting off to make another, and another, and another, flying by the seat of his pants, rarely stopping to reflect on how or why he makes the decisions he does.

Each of us is a little bit Claudia and a little bit Andrew. Our brains and the modes of thinking they enable often clash and collide as we try to make up our minds. In many ways, the duelling Claudia and Andrew model has served us quite well. After all, look at what we have built and how long we've managed to stick around as a species. On the other hand, look at what we have built and the looming threats to our survival. How have we managed to stick around?

Good question. Here are a few more. If the brain did not evolve for knowledge, if it is not a computer, if it is frequently overwhelmed, and if its various regions produce or process impulses often in conflict with one another, how is it that we ever get anything done? More to the point, how is that we have managed to progress from extremely precarious living conditions—humankind nearly went extinct around 70,000 BCE as our population dropped to a few thousand—to the world we live in today, in which hundreds of millions of us live long, stable, comfortable, healthy, and wealthy lives?[14] The answers to these questions are found in the story of the rise of social and political order, our environment, and the institutions and technologies that enable us to live in ways that were previously unimaginable.

In *Enlightenment 2.0*, philosopher Joseph Heath argues that we have a "peculiar genius" that we use for "colonizing the surrounding environment to augment our computational capacities."[15] Among our creations are tools and institutions for thinking, for sorting our world, and making our environment regular and predictable. Heath conceives of our tools and institutions as ways of projecting our reason outwards into the world, shaping it in such a way as to compensate for our cognitive shortcomings. His argument is convincing. After all, while few experts in the several fields that make up or interact with cognitive science dispute that our human cognition is imperfect and subject to bias, we still need to explain how we have managed to get so much done and to survive for millions of years.

Returning to Ronald Wright's Massey Lecture and book *A Short History of Progress*, we learn that while humans lack the physical evolutionary adaptations that would make us fierce hunters by virtue of our bodies—"We have no fangs, claws, or venom built into our bodies," he notes—we do have the brainpower necessary for inventing and using tools, for being able to abstract from things we see in our environment, and for making the items we find into something other than what they naturally are. As Wright continues, "Our specialization is the brain. The flexibility of the brain's interactions with nature, through culture, has been key to our success. Cultures can adapt far more quickly than genes to new threats and needs." Much like Heath, Wright sees the key to human success—and the danger of failure through missteps—in our ability to adapt to our environment and, indeed, to shape that environment through thinking. More specifically, we survive through our development and use of *ideas*—a practice that goes way, way, way back.[16]

I mean *way, way, way* back. The intellectual historian Peter Watson, in his book *Ideas: A History from Fire to Freud*, suggests that our earliest idea might have been to shape stone tools—and that notion stretches as far back as 2.5 million years.[17] Around that time, humans discovered that a rock, struck against another, would produce a tool that could be used to cut into the carcass of a dead animal. Our intellectual beginnings were, indeed, very humble. Yet they were sufficient to start a process that led to, among other accomplishments, modern medicine, flight, space travel, and the internet.

But lest you think that the rise of humankind is all about tools and technologies, we need to consider our less tangible inventions. Our story of survival and expansion also includes the rise of evolving norms, expectations, and rules. These guides have shaped our institutions and therefore our lives, giving us the solidity and predictability we need to make sense of the world. However, at the same time, they challenge us by pitting some of our drives, desires, and proclivities—some stretching back millions of years—against the normative demands of the social, cultural, and political systems that we have adopted.

Let's look at an example: lineups. This may seem trivial, or you might even despise them, but think about lines for a minute. When you need to get somewhere or get something done, your brain might say, "Just do it!" But you cannot "just do it." There are rules. Lineups, including queuing for a bus, waiting for a table at a restaurant, standing with others at a cashier, or getting ready to renew some piece of government identification help make our lives orderly. They also introduce fairness into what would otherwise be an unpredictable rush. As an extension of lineups, waiting lists also help make life easier to navigate, including more frivolous endeavours, such as being on the list to sign up for a race you want to run, or far more serious ones, such as waiting for an organ to become available for transplant. Norms, expectations, and rules are like beams we use to build sturdy and stable buildings, and they indicate something rather remarkable about our species: we can compensate for the shortcomings of our brains by *using our brains*.

One of the marvellous things about human beings is our ability to look at the world as it is and imagine it otherwise. This ability is not just for making stone axes or expecting people to line up. Think of how we have come to conceive of justice, fairness, punishment, redistribution, reward, and merit. We have taken these and other concepts and combined them in ways that have created institutions and systems that include elaborate rules, expectations, and procedures. But, because we are human and therefore flawed, that capacity also raises challenges, some of which are very serious.

Think of the dominant political system in the Western world: liberal democracy. In the eighteenth and nineteenth centuries, philosophers in the West developed a conception of political order that rested on increased suffrage, constitutionalism, and the rule of law. In a sense, liberal democracy is one big idea made up of many smaller ideas that are brought together to help us think about and decide on how to live together. But we have not evolved to think like this all the time. When it comes to *how* we think about and interact with our political system, things are very different than from how we approach simpler, more concrete ideas (such as the stone axe). Seeing a stone and imagining it as a tool for shaping the world around you is different from seeing a group of people and imagining a system in which they have inalienable rights and in which they, and you, are expected to take part in deciding how to live together.

Liberal democracy requires and expects certain things from its citizens —such as the ability to make autonomous and rational decisions—that we tend to under-deliver on, or fail to deliver on at all. In these instances, our cognitive capacities regularly let us down, exposing the gap between what we are asked to do and what we can do. Suddenly, in that moment we come up short. We realize that our expectations have outpaced our cognitive evolution. Our brains just can't always deliver what we want from them, or, worse, we get ahead of ourselves. When this occurs, we are vulnerable to making bad decisions that can get us into serious trouble. Indeed, occasionally the stakes are beyond high; for example, as Wright argues: "The atomic bomb, a logical progression from the arrow and the bullet, became the first technology to threaten our whole species with extinction."[18]

Sometimes the failure of a bad decision is our own fault—such as when we allow a bias or a hidden or uncontrolled emotional response to overtake our better judgment. In poker, the term *tilt* refers to when the way a game is going—whether you are playing well or poorly; whether you are lucky or unlucky—gets to you emotionally and affects how you play. The best poker players are good at adopting a strategy and adjusting it as needed based on the cards they are dealt, the opponents they are facing, and the shifting probabilities of them winning hand to hand. And they are good at sticking to their plan.

A player on tilt—for example, someone who has just lost a bunch of hands they expected to win and is aggressively trying to catch up to their expectations—is not one of those players. When a player is on tilt, the emotional brain takes over, and they make bad decisions, like betting a lot of money on a risky hand or playing hands with weak cards, despite their better judgment. If you've ever played poker, or any game or sport, and had a run of bad luck, there's a good chance you know exactly what I'm talking about.

The example of a poker player spinning out because of bad luck is an instance of failure driven by the person themselves. At other times, this failure is engineered by others, such as when misleading advertising or digital manipulation lures you into making a decision that you wouldn't otherwise make. Examples of this abound in politics.

In 2016, British voters elected to leave the European Union. The Brexit referendum process has been shrouded in controversy, with allegations that some on the Leave side engaged in dodgy spending practices and collusion with foreign entities (for instance, the group Leave.EU, supported by British politician Nigel Farage). These concerns have made spectacular headlines. But somewhat more quietly, the integrity of the vote may also have been compromised by botnets, an online network of connected devices that exist to perform some coordinated task or series of tasks. In October 2017, researchers Marco T. Bastos and Dan Mercea from City, University of London uncovered a network of Twitterbots that were in operation during the Brexit campaign but disappeared after the vote was finished, either because they were deactivated by their owners or removed by Twitter (since their paper was published, Twitter confirmed that it deleted 71 per cent of the accounts in the botnet). The two found a collection of 13,493 accounts that tilted towards supporting the Vote Leave side, tweeting dubious content "much akin to hyper partisan tabloid journalism," as Bastos and Mercea put it.[19]

Bots and botnets can mislead or manipulate internet users by flooding online spaces with questionable if not outright false information, by amplifying the message of one side or another to make its position seem more popular than it is, or by forcing that position to the front of people's minds—hijacking their overloaded brains. Somewhat reassuringly, the researchers found that in this case the bots played a very minor role in the referendum. But, they warned, "The hyper-partisan content pushed by the botnet epitomizes an ongoing trend to push viral content that is mostly short, shareable, accessible with mobile devices, and that accentuates polarized identities and balkanizes readerships into like-minded groups."

Manipulative campaign ads are now standard practice, online and offline, as spin doctors and other political actors try to exploit the unconscious or emotional brain. The use of music, images, and melodramatic voiceovers to make emotional appeals has been the gold standard on TV and radio for years, but the internet is now home to new and frightening ways of leading voters astray. Ads rarely seek to make a rational argument. Instead, they are designed to bypass rational consideration and focus directly on emotional appeals to voters. Even in cases where an advertisement attempts to persuade through reason and rational appeal, some emotive element is usually included, meant to work behind the scenes and often even outside of your awareness.

Today, with the internet, social media, and increasingly sophisticated techniques emerging from neuroscience and psychology research, manipulation is a bigger threat than ever before. But it is not a *new* threat. During the 1993 Canadian federal election, the Progressive Conservative Party put this strategy to the test. Trailing in the polls and beleaguered by a weak economy and national malaise, the Tories decided to launch a television advertisement that attacked Liberal Party leader Jean Chrétien. The ad focused on a close-up of Chrétien's face while a voiceover asked, "Is this a prime minister?" It showed several images of Chrétien, whose face is partially paralyzed as a result of Bell's palsy, while the narrator attacked the Liberal leader as unfit to be prime minister. The ad generated public backlash, in part encouraged by the Liberal Party, who saw an opportunity to cast the Tories as mean-spirited and desperate. While the Progressive Conservatives were already in trouble heading into the election, the ad did not help. They finished in fifth place, dropping a staggering 169 seats (down to two) and losing nearly 2.2 million votes. Even their leader, Prime Minister Kim Campbell, lost her seat.

The lesson from what has become known as "the face ad" is that appeals to emotion or gut assessment are risky, since you cannot always predict what someone's reaction is going to be. While the Tories sought to sow the seeds of doubt by appealing to a sense that Chrétien *didn't look like a prime minister*, they instead seemed to generate disgust at what was seen as a personal attack outside the boundaries of good taste. But was the ad bound to be a failure?

Political strategist Warren Kinsella, in *Kicking Ass in Canadian Politics*, quotes former Tory fixer-turned-senator Hugh Segal, who suggests the biggest mistake the Tories made was pulling that ad—a view echoed by pollster Allan Gregg, who served as a senior pollster and communications manager during the 1993 contest.[20] The two of them might be on to something. While distasteful ads might offend, that does not mean that they are not effective. Sometimes it just takes a little time for a narrative to form — time for the emotional part of our brains to accept and internalize the narrative intended by an ad or a series of ads.

When Trump, as a candidate and later as president, repeats lies about illegal immigration (far less of a problem than he claims), massive voter fraud (which does not occur in the United States), spiking crime rates (crime is declining), and the "lyin'" press (the media is not perfect, but very few of its members lie about their work), he is shaping a narrative that certain Americans — his base — come to believe, out of ignorance. The *accuracy* of the message is not as important as the *feelings* the message is meant to induce: in these instances, anger or fear.

In the United States, few ads are as infamous as the 1988 Willie Horton spot. Horton, a convicted felon, was released on furlough (from which he did not return) in Massachusetts in 1986. While out of prison, he committed rape and assault. During the 1988 presidential election, Republican candidate and future president George H.W. Bush tied support of the furlough program to his Democratic opponent, Michael Dukakis. In the ad, Bush and Dukakis are contrasted on crime. Bush is presented as supporting the death penalty for first-degree murder, while Dukakis...well, as the ad ran: "Dukakis not only opposes the death penalty, he allowed first-degree murderers to have weekend passes from prison." As the narrator concludes this sentence, Willie Horton's face comes into view as the felon's crimes are listed and viewers are reminded of his furlough. The ad finishes with the words "Weekend prison passes, Dukakis on crime" spoken by the narrator and appearing on the screen. The ad was criticized for being racist and demeaning. It did nothing for civic discourse. In fact, it was so offensive that its creator, Lee Atwater, later regretted it and, while dying of cancer, apologized for running it. But it worked. It captured millions of emotional brains, consciously or unconsciously, and put them to work for the Republican cause. And while it set a new low for political advertising, it also reminded us that fear and implicit association can be disturbingly successful.

When manipulative ads influence how we think about a candidate or how we vote, we are witnessing the effects of the gap I mentioned earlier between *how we imagine ourselves to be* and *how we tend to be* with regard to our physiology, our psychology, our environment, and our institutions—which all link back to our messy brains, what they make possible, and how they make us vulnerable. The bad news is that it is common for this gap to emerge and to get in the way of good decisions—and it is extremely common for it to be exploited in politics. The good news, however, is that we can do better. We can improve our own behaviour and our common institutions to bring what we tend to do closer in line with what we are expected to do.

The even better news is that if we do this, we will start making better political decisions. And that will help us tackle the social and political challenges we face individually and collectively.

2. Deciding in democracies:
The long road to self-government

The story of how and why we make good or bad political decisions is also the story of the context in which we make them. You cannot separate a decision from the time and place in which it is made. Our personalities and brains, our environment and the institutions within which we think, what information is available to us, what we pay attention to, and a panoply of incentives and disincentives guide us towards one option or another.

Today, the context in which most of us make political decisions will be as citizens of a liberal democracy—a historically remarkable form of government premised on individual rights and freedoms, elected representation, and the rule of law. I say "historically remarkable" because "weird" seems uncharitable. But "weird" works, too. Throughout most of human history, countries as we know them did not exist, and the political entities into which we organized ourselves were not democratic. The idea that "the people" should rule themselves, that they should decide, is a radical one. In fact, if you were to go through each year of human history and mark it as democratic or undemocratic, the count would not even be close.

So how did we get here? The answer to this question lies in a story that takes us all the way back to the Neolithic Revolution, when humans domesticated animals and crops and adopted a sedentary lifestyle. As soon as we decided to stay put, new problems arose, including figuring out how to live side-by-side in settled communities, how to tackle new diseases, how to manage food supplies, and how to deal with theft ("Hey, Larry, that's *my* obsidian!"). These challenges required new institutions and approaches to organizing collective life and, over time, also required new sorts of leaders to manage them. As life grew more complex, so did our practices and rules. What started as simple hunter-gatherer life eventually led to the electoral college, door knocking, robocalls, databases, sophisticated ads, and debates over how much time a candidate should spend shaking hands and kissing babies in Saskatchewan.

Democracy was not our destiny. It was not written in the stars that we would govern ourselves. It is the product of a long history of contingent changes to how we think and how we collectively decide how to live together. The story of how we came to be citizens—deciders—is epic and far from linear. Like Odysseus, whose route from Troy back home to Ithaca was, let's say, circuitous, so too has been our journey to democracy.

My focus in this book is on Western democracy in Europe and North America, so the "we" that I am speaking of is narrowed from about 7.6 billion people to around 1.3 billion. Moreover, the history of our political organization as an evolution from small tribal bands to mass bureaucratic democracy does not fully capture the many varieties of order that have existed throughout the world since we started walking on two feet. Nonetheless, there is a story to tell here in broad strokes, one that takes us from small, disconnected bands of kin-based peoples to tribes, monarchies, and empires, onwards to feudal fiefdoms, back to monarchies and empires, and then along to democracies—which themselves continue to evolve.

The bulk of human history took place in the Paleolithic Era. This "Old Stone Age" was prehistoric—prior to the invention of written records— and stretched from the time when hominids began to use tools, about 2.5 million years ago (maybe earlier), up to around ten thousand years ago at the end of the Pleistocene, the last "Ice Age." This was the family-and-band era of the human story, a time of small groups of nomadic hunter-gatherer-scavengers struggling to survive in an inhospitable environment that included megafauna, such as the wooly mammoth, the glyptodon (an armadillo the size of a small car), and the megalodon (an ocean predator that could grow to nearly sixty feet and featured teeth that were up to seven inches long).[1]

There is not much to be said about political decision-making during the Paleolithic Era. What we know of the time comes from anthropologists and archaeologists who reconstruct what life might have been like for prehistoric peoples by observing existing hunter-gatherer peoples and drawing inferences or examining fossils and objects that have survived.[2] It is safe to say that political decision-making in early human history would have been a much simpler affair than it would later become, even if the day-to-day stakes of every decision—an immediate matter of life or death—were higher. Although, in our hunter-gatherer days, folks could, as it is often put, "vote with their feet." If you were not happy with your arrangement, you could leave.

At some point, however, humans discovered a more fixed way of living and our relationships to each another and to forms of political organization slowly became more complicated. Archaeologist Steven Mithen summarizes this transition in his hefty and wonderfully readable volume *After the Ice: A Global Human History, 20,000-5,000 BC*:

> Little of significance happened until 20,000 BC—
> people simply continued living as hunter-gatherers, just
> as their ancestors had been doing for millions of years.
> They lived in small communities and never remained
> within one settlement for very long...then came an
> astonishing 15,000 years that saw the origin of farming,
> towns, and civilization. By 5,000 BC the foundations
> of the modern world had been laid and nothing that
> came after—classical Greece, the Industrial Revolution,
> the atomic age, the Internet—has ever matched the
> significance of those events.[3]

This was the Neolithic Revolution. And it all started once we *stopped*. Once human beings settled, trading our nomadic lifestyle for permanent settlements, our relationship to one another and to how we live together started to change. It is not entirely clear why humans gave up their hunter-gatherer lives, since contrary to what you might expect, in some ways nomadic lifestyles suited people quite well (for instance, we did not live cheek by jowl with livestock, which helped us avoid picking up certain diseases). But for whatever reason, we did give it up. Though still tribal, sedentary life required new ways of living together — new norms and new institutions. Even with the arrival of the Neolithic Revolution, we were still a long way from states and democracy. But the domestication of plants and animals along with permanent settlements set humankind on a path that would make these forms of political organization possible.

Increasingly complex societies soon found that they needed new ways to decide on matters of collective interest, mechanisms to settle disputes, norms for managing personal relationships, methods for keeping track of goods, and even specialists for taking care of the sorts of routine affairs that accompany life in permanent settlements. In these basic requirements for settled life we find the seeds and soil that would eventually sprout popular assemblies, laws, property, and specialized professions.

There is no single formula for the transformation from hunter-gatherer-scavenger to settlement and later to state. The story of the rise of India is different from that of China, which is different still from the story of the rise of Europe — and certainly different from the North American tale. But these changes occurred throughout the world over the course of many years.

A lot happened in the time between the Neolithic Revolution and the birth of institutional European democracy. During those millennia in Europe (and elsewhere), settlements gave rise to towns and cities, permanent or semi-permanent rulers took charge of city states and proto-empires, religion grew more sophisticated, art and culture became more refined, a system of law and order emerged, and we became more talented at waging war on one another. These developments took thousands of years. Yet we have little more than scattered records of primitive democracy until a few city states in Greece, beginning in the seventh century BCE, adopted forms of self-government, including, most famously, Athens.

We often refer to Athens as the birthplace of democracy, but the pioneering Greeks of the ancient city state practised a form of it very different from our own. Athenian democracy was direct: citizens debated and voted directly on laws. Also, participation was limited to adult citizens, and citizenship itself was restricted to free Athenian-born males. Those who could actively participate accounted for about 10 to 15 per cent of the overall population of Athens—a far cry from mass democracy as we know it today, even if our representative form of government asks little of us (in our democracy, we elect people to pass laws and policies for us rather than do it ourselves by showing up to an assembly or holding referendums all the time).[4]

Even with constraints on who could take part in governing, with Athens we reached a critical juncture, one at which humankind started down a path that would eventually take us on a long journey from early democracy practised by the few along the rocky shores of Greece to the many casting ballots in Kamloops, Springfield, and Weymouth.

The story of that journey reveals a slow lurching towards more inclusive and sophisticated institutions that required increasingly refined decision-making capacities without much by way of cognitive update. Imagine that our lives are a piece of software. Now imagine that our bodies, and especially our brains, are the hardware on which we run that software. Over the last tens of thousands of years, and especially in the last few thousand years, we have asked our hardware to tackle increasingly complicated tasks required to run the software. Yet we have not had a major hardware upgrade in that time. Like a computer that has been asked by its user to do too much, too quickly, we can freeze and not function properly. Our brains get locked in the spinning wheel of death.

As a result, ours is not a history of uninterrupted and inevitable progress.

Our story is, at best, a long, rambling sentence of whirls and swirls and moments of triumph and shame that has arrived at a semicolon that risks becoming a full stop. We seem to be under the impression that we have solved the problems of history, that we have reached the final level and now it is merely a matter of enjoying our triumph while we fidget with our new gadgets. History cautions us to be humbler.

Athenian democracy rose in the sixth century BCE, flourished for a little under two hundred years (with a brief interruption by a Spartan-backed oligarchy after the Peloponnesian War), and fell to Philip of Macedon, father of Alexander the Great, in the late fourth century BCE. To some extent, the rise of Rome returned some democratic governance but nothing quite like Athens in its glory days.

Rome coexisted with Athens in the ancient world, its tenure stretching from its founding in the eighth century BCE until its fall in the fifth century CE, but not before it had "engulfed all the old Hellenistic Greek World," as Paul Cartledge, a classicist at the University of Cambridge, puts it.[5] Rome flourished as a sort of democracy in which Roman citizens—*Cives Romani*—took part in political life, for a while. I say "for a while" because democracy in Rome did not last long. In the Eternal City, a kingdom became a republic, only to later become an empire that collapsed upon itself and took much of the "known" world down with it. The fall of Rome and the beginning of the early medieval era, marked as it was by decentralization and the absence of democracy, serves as a reminder that our institutions are not immortal, that the law of life is change, decay, and death.

While the Roman republic and its institutions lived, however, they took up the mantle of self-government that had been left vacant by Greece. But Rome was never democratic in the same way that Greece was. The republic, which began in 509 BCE after Romans deposed the last of their kings, Tarquin the Proud, *technically* lasted until 27 BCE. That was the year Octavian was granted the title Augustus to complement his title of imperator, twenty-two years after Caesar crossed the Rubicon and seventeen years after the Senate declared him dictator for life (though not king).[6] The Romans did not like the idea of being ruled by kings. In fact, in Antiquity, *republic* referred to a political body that was not ruled by a king. Yet the title *dictator* had a long and more palatable pedigree in Rome. Just eight years after the founding of the republic, in response to a military crisis, Rome appointed its first dictator.

Back then, the position of dictator was not inconsistent with democratic government—at least not in the way that Romans practised democracy. As Bauer puts it:

> The office of dictator was not, as in modern times, license
> for unlimited power. The Roman dictators had power
> for only six months at a time, and had to be appointed
> by the ruling consuls. Often the dictator *was* one of the
> consuls. His role was to keep Rome secure in the face of
> extraordinary outside threats, but he also had unusual
> powers inside the city. Consuls were allowed to impose the
> death penalty on Romans outside the walls of Rome...
> but inside Rome they had to submit criminals to the will
> of the voting population for punishment. The dictator,
> though, was allowed to exercise that power of life and
> death inside Rome itself, with no obligation to consult
> the people.

Bauer also notes that "implicit obedience" was Rome's "first defense," and while the rights of the republic were *first* "suspended for the sake of expediency" in 501 BCE, that wouldn't be the final time extraordinary powers were assumed.[7] So, like its Greek progenitor, Roman democracy was constrained, but in different ways. The propensity to strictly and expansively limit democratic and other rights in times of crisis was one way, but there were others. Cartledge argues that "there was an essential popular dimension to Roman Republic self-governance and decision-making."[8] It was anti-tyranny and anti-king. But he hastens to add that the elite-led Senate dominated Roman political life during the republican era over the plebeian-elected Tribunes of the Plebs. And votes for elected positions—magistrates and tribunes—were cast by *group* and not on the basis of one man, one vote, with which we are familiar (expanded more recently to the more inclusive one *person*, one vote). Romans also owned slaves, who had neither voting rights nor political representation. As Cartledge notes, "the group method systematically favoured the rich few," and while Roman citizenship was open to many—far more than the Greeks—few outside the city could travel to Rome to participate.[9] At best, Roman democracy was an elite-led, quasi-timocratic (government by property owners) affair.

Yet Roman citizens, like their Greek forebears, played *some* role in political decision-making: on taxes, foreign policy, war, and more mundane affairs. And they did a fine enough job for a long time. The republic leveraged a political system based on checks and balances, some measure of meaningful inclusiveness, and a deep sense of civic duty to grow and flourish. But the republic fell, just as the empire would after it.

Why did the republic fall? And the empire? There are plenty of theories that try to answer each of those questions, but economists Daron Acemoglu and James A. Robinson tell a compelling story that relates the decline and fall of the republic and empire to one another and to a general theory of why political entities collapse. In *Why Nations Fail*, they argue that Roman economic growth was based on unsustainable, extractive institutions in which a small group exploited a larger group for material gain.[10] Or, to put it differently, Rome operated under a system in which important decisions were made by the few and in which everyone else was left out.

Over time, these parasitic institutions became too prevalent, inequality too widespread, and elite domination too entrenched. (Sound familiar?) Reforms failed, and they failed in a *very* old-fashioned way. When the tribune—a representative of ordinary Romans—Tiberius Gracchus tried to level the playing field by introducing land reforms, he was *beaten to death by senators*, and his corpse was tossed into the Tiber River.

Gracchus's reform attempts and consequent murder occurred roughly one hundred years before the republic fell, thus serving as both a last-ditch effort to save and then later an epitaph for Roman democracy.

Rome's decline led to changes in social, political, economic, and cultural life in Europe and beyond. From the ashes of a smoldering empire grew coercive and exploitative feudal institutions. Democratic Athens had included few in political decision-making, but it included them deeply. Republican Rome included many, but more shallowly. Feudal Europe included almost no one in decision-making, with some notable but minor exceptions from around the seventh century onwards in parts of England, Iberia, Iceland, and elsewhere.

It would be a hit job to dismiss the thousand years of European history that followed the fall of Rome as merely the Dark Ages, a long pause in the history of human development, or, worse, a long press on the rewind button. But politically, the years from the fifth century up until about the seventeenth century did not contain much democratic progress. In fact, for hundreds and hundreds of years *democracy* was a foul word. If it was spoken at all, it referred to mob rule.

During these years, the centralizing force of the Roman Empire was replaced by the decentralizing consequences of its collapse. Small kingdoms and city states emerged, some of which included proto-democratic institutions, such as the merchant guilds of the Italian peninsula. But in general, this was a time of the creeping return of autocratic government. Feudalism and oligarchy created space for the rise of absolutist monarchs. Yet by the seventeenth century, we are beginning to talk about states, which is a big deal.

In 1648, the Peace of Westphalia was concluded. This collection of treaties ended wars over religion and territory and power that had raged for decades and confirmed the state system. It also entrenched the idea that political entities have ultimate authority—sovereignty—over the territory they govern. In the seventeenth century that sovereignty, belonging to the state, was vested in the monarch. (Louis XIV's famous "L'état, c'est moi.") The history of modern democracy, and the history of democratic political decision-making, is the history of the transfer of sovereignty from a God-approved monarch to the people, either directly (in a republic) or indirectly (in a constitutional monarchy).

And so we arrive at our own time, in which we are asked to make political decisions. We had to struggle, fight, and literally kill to get that sacred right. But in a cruel twist, we are not always equipped or prepared to exercise this right as well as we might hope to.

Danish philosopher Søren Kierkegaard explained a lot of history when he wrote (or at least as he's commonly paraphrased)[11]: "Life can only be understood backwards; but it must be lived forwards." At the dawn of the eighteenth century no one could have predicted that in a hundred years the face of Europe and North America would be dramatically remade with citizens at the centre. In 1700, France was under absolutist rule and "America" was still two short of the thirteen colonies that would become the United States of America. By 1800, the French and American revolutions had been fought. The United States quickly established representative—though qualified and limited—democracy. France was molded and remolded like clay between 1789 and 1958 from a kingdom into a republic, an empire, a monarchy once again, a republic once more, an empire a second time around, a third republic, a split into free and Vichy France during the Second World War, a provisional republic, a fourth republic, and, finally, into the fifth republic that stands today. But the French Revolution of 1789-99 had set the country on a path towards democracy that, winding though it was, would encourage other states to pursue democratic self-determination and self-rule.

By the late eighteenth century, after hundreds of years of lying dormant, democracy was awake again. At the centre of the democratic impulse was the idea that *the people* were ultimately sovereign, naturally endowed with the right to decide for themselves how they ought to live together. Not monarchs. Not emperors. *The people.* And that idea was spreading. In 1848, a series of greater and lesser reform movements, re-volts, and revolutions swept across Europe—in France (again), Austria, Hungary, Ireland, the Italian and German states, Denmark, Poland, Belgium, the Netherlands, and elsewhere. Meanwhile, democracy in England and some of its territories, including Canada, plodded along, developing slowly, but steadily enough. The old European and colonial political order's foundations were becoming increasingly unstable.

Just 242 years separate 1776 and 2018. Yet in the short time between widespread democratic restlessness in Europe and the global spread of (primarily) liberal democracy, more changed about how we live together than at any other time in human history, save for perhaps the Neolithic Revolution. The First World War unmade and made states, giving a boost to the prospects of democracy in the process. Changes in the 1930s and the Second World War undid some of that work. But in the aftermath of German, Italian, and Japanese defeats, democracy was on the rise again. Along with the decolonization movements beginning in the 1950s, a wave of democratization swept the planet and the number of democratic countries skyrocketed, as it would again with a new or "Third Wave" in the 1990s, after the fall of the Soviet Union. By 2018, roughly 120 of 192 states were democracies, depending on how you count. That said, in recent years, threats to democracy have returned, challenging popular self-government in some places where democracy is newer, including in Hungary and Poland, and some democratic stalwarts, such as the United States.

Growing threats to democracy remind us that history is not linear and progress is neither inevitable not irreversible. Not only is any progress we have made a waypoint on a long and winding road, but it is also marked by detours and dead ends. Of course it is still tempting to outline "stages" of history as I have just done and accept the idea that we move through them, one by one, as if we were climbing rungs on a ladder.

My copy of Johan Norberg's 2016 book *Progress* is bright yellow. On the cover is a graph and, in the middle, a simple image of a smile.

The subtitle of the book is *Ten reasons to look forward to the future*. As promised, Norberg tells ten good-news stories about the future, each one its own chapter: food, sanitation, life expectancy, poverty, violence, the environment, literacy, freedom, equality, and the new generation. But Norberg writes about progress, he notes, as much as a warning against complacency as a celebration of success.[12]

I take that warning seriously—and then some. I am more pessimistic about our future than he is or, perhaps, more concerned that the tectonic shifts that are occurring right now are not routine adjustments but an indication that a massive earthquake is coming, just as it came for the Greeks and the Romans and others before us. When we lean on the progress narrative, we find that it does not quite hold up. Climate change is the single most significant challenge humankind has faced in the last several thousand years, at least in recorded history. It is an existential threat. The proliferation of nuclear weapons is another risk to our species and the planet. Hundreds of millions remain in poverty and slavery, violence has declined but remains a threat to countless people around the world, and the progress we have made threatens to be lost amidst political unraveling and democratic backsliding. While many treat human rights and democracy as achievements that, once unlocked, are permanent, the rise of far-right movements in Europe and North America are startling reminders that this is not necessarily true.

And, alarmingly, it is not only extremists who are a threat to democracy. In the United States, a 2017 Pew Research poll found that 22 per cent of respondents claimed that autocracy—rule by a single individual with total power—was a "total good" and 17 per cent rated military government so, though only 13 per cent said representative democracy was a "total bad." In Canada, the numbers were 17 per cent for autocracy, 10 per cent for the military, and 10 per cent opposed to representative democracy. In Europe, support for autocratic rule was higher, with significant percentages of the population supporting it in Italy (29 per cent), the United Kingdom (26 per cent), and Hungary (24 per cent), though support for military rule was more muted: Italy (17 per cent), France (17 per cent), the United Kingdom (15 per cent). Worldwide, support for representative democracy was strong (78 per cent good versus 17 per cent bad), though rule by a strong leader (autocracy) gained 26 per cent support. Rule by the military also had robust backing (24 per cent).[13] Far too many people doubt the value of democracy.

Recent books about democratic decline in the United States and around the world, such as David Runciman's *How Democracy Ends*, Cass Sunstein's edited volume *Can It Happen Here?*, and political scientists Steven Levitsky and Daniel Ziblatt's *How Democracies Die*, pick up on a growing sense that democratic government is under threat—especially as Russia deepens its commitment to authoritarianism and China offers a non-democratic, quasi-capitalist alternative.[14] Researcher and UN special adviser Jennifer Welsh has even gone so far as to declare *The Return of History*. She warns of cracks in the foundation of liberal democracy and "the reappearance of trends and practices many believed had been erased: arbitrary executions, attempts to annihilate ethnic and religious minorities, the starvation of besieged populations, invasion and annexation of territory, and the mass movement of refugees and displaced persons."[15]

I mention these threats to democracy and stability as the flipside of Norberg's *Progress* and others who hail our accomplishments without sufficient regard for the fact that we are squandering them. I also mention them as a call to more inclusion in self-government, because the cure for the ills of democracy is *more democracy*.

If we had to govern ourselves with only what we could remember and easily retrieve from our brains, we would be in trouble fast. Writing—the ultimate technology for storing things outside of ourselves—was invented around 3500 BCE by the Sumerians so that they would not have to keep so much in their heads when engaging in business and trade, and so that they had reliable records to facilitate exchange. It was not long before writing was incorporated into governing. That is what we, as humans, do. We invent systems and we use them to make our lives easier. That is the secret to our success.

At its most basic, a system is a way of doing things that may include several elements—such as instructions, rules, and so forth—depending on what kind of system it is. An institution is a common part of a system. It is also a *social structure* that governs collective behaviour. In turn, collective behaviour is a settled pattern of rules by which we abide—more or less, anyway.

I am going to talk about institutions a lot, and to make things easier I am going to lump systems in with them. There are differences between the two, but they are similar enough to one another that for my purposes it is close enough for jazz.

Over centuries, millennia in some cases, we have slowly and painstakingly constructed institutions to solve our most fundamental problem: the fact that we are human and constrained by the limits of our biology and psychology. We are okay at it. But since we are humans, as flawed as we are impressive, as unwise as we are clever, we make mistakes. We are constantly searching for a solution to a problem that we have encountered in nature or constructed for ourselves. Too often we come up with an answer that improves our lives but simultaneously creates serious, new problems.

Consider juries. The right to be tried by a jury of your peers is a major legal development stretching back to Ancient Greece and is common today throughout the world. It's an important legal institution. The idea behind such a trial is that it prevents the abuse of state power— of overreach or discrimination—and so it protects citizens by ensuring equal treatment before the law. But at the same time, it exposes certain types of accused people to the prejudices of their peers, replacing possible state injustices with possible injustices of ordinary citizens.

In her paper "Studying the Effects of Race, Ethnicity, and Culture on Jury Behaviour," psychologist Jennifer Hunt explores the ways that what should be irrelevant considerations—like the colour of a person's skin —affect the administration of justice. She argues that race and ethnicity impact trials in all kinds of ways, including what kind of juries are selected in the first place (meaning that sometimes defendants don't *actually* get a jury that could be reasonably thought of as their peers) and how those juries think about and judge the defendant. For instance, she suggests that a look into the archives of death penalty cases in America reveals that jurors give the death penalty to black or Latino defendants who have been convicted of killing a white person more often than the reverse.[16]

In Canada, the Colten Boushie case brought the issue of jury bias and racial injustice to the forefront of many people's minds. In 2016, Gerald Stanley fatally shot the twenty-two-year-old Indigenous man after Boushie and his friends drove onto Stanley's Saskatchewan farm. Stanley was charged with second-degree murder. The case was controversial from the beginning. Stanley claimed he had merely fired warning shots to scare off the visitors, and that the bullet that killed Boushie was accidentally fired—"hang fired," as his lawyer, Scott Spencer, suggested, a malfunction that occurs when there's a delay between pulling the trigger and the bullet being fired.

In February 2018, a jury made up solely of jurors who appeared to be white acquitted Stanley of second-degree murder. Stanley was also found not guilty of the lesser offence of manslaughter. During the jury selection process, prospective Indigenous jurors were included in the jury pool but were rejected by Stanley's lawyers using peremptory challenges—a set number of vetoes that lawyers can use in a criminal trial to exclude someone from sitting on the jury without needing to give any reason why. There has been a lot of debate about whether peremptory challenges were used in this case to systematically exclude Indigenous people from serving on Stanley's jury and whether a jury that included visibly Indigenous jurors would have returned the same verdict. As University of Toronto law professor Kent Roach said at the time: "Peremptory challenges... are really an invitation to discrimination."[17]

Nonetheless, even though some institutions are flawed and need to change, we rely on them all the time, and we do not have much of a choice—we cannot live without them.

As a system of government, democracy is full of institutions: constitutions, the rule of law, elections and majority rule, political parties, and even the news media. Each of these institutions is the product of centuries of development, and they have enabled us to live together in moderate peace and prosperity. Our political institutions set rules that are meant to make democratic life inclusive, fair, and predictable. We can argue over how much they have succeeded at each of these functions, but the point is that those are their general functions, and they tend to fulfill them, which is good, since for democracy to work, these institutions require buy-in from the population. People need to believe their institutions are working for them, and they need to take part in them. For democracy that means that we should vote, moderately competent folks need to stand for election (and win, at least sometimes), human rights must be respected, the news media must remain independent and critical, and citizens and residents need to obey the constitution and abide by the rule of law.

On the face of it, none of this seems like too much to ask of people. It seems reasonable that we act decently, that we think a little bit about what we want and expect as citizens, that we contribute to our democracy through service, and that, hopefully, we stay informed about what is happening around us. But under the surface lies a radical idea that entails an equally radical commitment from those of us who live under it: We, the people, not only *get to* decide but we *must* decide.

In other words, in liberal democracies the masses are not just permitted to participate in self-government, they are *expected* to participate in it. Now, I hear footsteps behind me. The critics are rushing to point out that not everyone is, in fact, included, that democracies include systemic alienation. Yes, absolutely. Democracies in North America and Europe (and elsewhere) that claim to be universal are far from it, and each includes varying degrees of haunting past, and inexcusable present, exclusion. But liberal democracies have nonetheless included in law and achieved in practice a combined scope and scale of democratic inclusiveness never achieved in human history. Flawed, yes. In need of very serious improvement, if not radical uprooting, yes. Unprecedented, also yes.

In fact, that is my point: nothing we have achieved implies that everything is fine or that the good bits are here to stay no matter what. I have turned on the lights, now let me dim them. For democracy to survive, citizens must take part in the system — by voting, participating in town halls, writing or calling their representative, learning about and discussing issues — and they need to trust their institutions. Democracy does not just *happen* — it is an ongoing project that requires that we set ambitious goals and standards for ourselves and then live up to them.

My argument in this book is that *we absolutely can* live up to these standards, but *the world around us often sets us up for failure, in part by exploiting the limits of our brains and minds*. To illustrate this, I want to highlight some of the indicators that decisions that we, including our leaders, have made suggest that there is trouble in democratic paradise.

First, trust. In 2017, the year Edelman's Trust Barometer named Trust in Crisis, the firm found a widening trust gap between what they call the "informed population" — who are older, college educated, top earners, avid business-media consumers — and the broader population — folks who, for whatever reason, are less informed about the ins and outs of the day-to-day news. The chasm between the two varied from country to country, but it hit eighteen points in France, nineteen points in the United Kingdom, and twenty-one points in the United States. The informed population is more trusting than the mass population (who make up 87 per cent of the global population), but those numbers are not particularly encouraging either: on average 60 per cent of the former trust institutions versus 45 per cent of the latter. Researchers found that people distrust their institutions in democracies including the United States, Canada, Italy, Spain, Australia, Germany, France, the United Kingdom, Sweden,

Ireland, and Poland. Sadly, 2017 was a year of a notable and widespread decline in trust, with levels in twenty-one of twenty-eight countries dropping.[18] Weak trust numbers might help explain the Pew study I cited earlier; as trust in institutions declines, citizens are starting to look around at alternatives to democracy.

Trust in the media is also in decline, reaching an all-time low in seventeen countries. In 82 per cent of the countries surveyed, more people distrust the media than trust it. Trust in government also declined, as well as in non-governmental organizations. Perhaps most disconcerting of all: a full half of countries surveyed had populations who had "lost faith in the system," with the loss of faith most prevalent in Western-style democracies, including the United States, Canada, the United Kingdom, and France.

Second, voting. Democracy is much more than voting, but casting a ballot in a free and fair election is essential to representative democracy. For years, voter turnout has been declining throughout the world. The 2017 *World Development Report* from the World Bank found that worldwide voter turnout declined by over 10 per cent since 1945.[19] In the United States, the 2016 presidential election hit a twenty-year turnout low at 55 per cent — though it has traditionally had low turnout, at an average of about 57 per cent. In Canada, turnout has been in steady decline since the 1960s. In 1963, 79 per cent of eligible voters cast a ballot; in 1993, the number had dropped to 69.6 per cent, a rate that hasn't been reached again since — though 2015 came close at 68.5 per cent. In the United Kingdom, turnout has also been in decline since the 1980s, with a particularly stunning drop between 1992 (77.7 per cent) and 2001 (59.4 per cent), though 2017 was a banner year, reaching nearly 69 per cent. Even with the occasional surge in turnout, fewer citizens are participating in elections overall.

While one explanation is that this trend reflects satisfaction with the status quo — democracy: set it and forget it! — the decline in trust challenges that claim. Declining turnout poses a risk to representative policy outcomes, since politicians have an incentive to deliver the goods to voters and to ignore non-voters. For instance, voter turnout in Canada skews older. As I mentioned, 2015 was an exceptional election driven in part by the youthful energy brought to the contest by Liberal leader Justin Trudeau. Youth turnout (voters aged eighteen to twenty-four) went up a whopping 39 per cent. But even then only 57 per cent of young people cast their ballot. In the same election, older voters (aged sixty-five to seventy-four) turned out in droves, with 80 per cent of them voting.[20] With the sheer force of their turnout numbers, senior citizens in Canada have a profound effect on not only who wins elections but what kinds of policies candidates and parties offer. A 2015 study found that governments spend up to *four times more* on social spending for Canadians over sixty-five as they do on those under forty-five.[21] Even when considering that health costs associated with aging are expensive, the concerns of young people are under-represented in spending.

Poor government responsiveness and policy representation could drive turnout even lower, further sink trust levels, and contribute to social and political inequality—all of which are bad news for the long-term viability of representative democracy—as citizens turn away from a system that they perceive as failing to serve their needs and interests. And while it is easy to say that decisions are made by those who show up or that if you do not vote, you do not get to complain, if people cannot see themselves and their concerns represented in government, it is hard to blame them for checking out and focusing on their day-to-day concerns. Once the cycle of decline in turnout and trust starts, it is hard to reverse it, and that is bad news for all of us, including those who regularly cast their ballot, trust government, and feel that they are served by policies.

If trust continues to decline, if citizens continue to ignore their democratic duty, and if a crisis or series of crises suddenly strikes—mass migration due to climate change, weather disasters, an epidemic, a massive war, a nuclear event—democratic systems could soon find themselves disintegrating. Your temptation might be to say, understandably, "It could never happen here!" In Europe and North America, millions of us have lived in peace and prosperity for decades. But I am sure that plenty of ancient Athenians and republican Romans felt the same way. History does not excuse political decay just because a political body happens to be democratic.

To resist democratic decline and collapse, we need to take a greater role in self-government. That is a tad tricky, but it's not impossible. As it stands, democracies simultaneously ask very little and a lot of their citizens. They ask very little in the sense that citizens are usually tasked merely with casting an occasional ballot (which many of us do not bother to do), thinking about and discussing the occasional political issue (ditto), respecting the rule of law, paying our taxes, and perhaps serving on a jury. They ask a lot in the sense that when we *are* asked to engage in political thinking—considering issues around an election before we cast our vote, paying attention to the news coverage and party platforms to be able to form or express a political opinion, writing a letter to the editor, or some other kind of political engagement—we are asked to shift into a mode of thinking that is taxing, and we are asked to do it in surroundings that are often inhospitable to the task. We may not be motivated or trained to think in this way, and it upsets our default (and typically preferred) cognitive mode: autopilot.

Democracy calls each of us to do something that we have not specifically evolved to do: engage in complex and often abstract reasoning about issues that may or may not directly affect us. While humans have the capacity to meet these challenges in at least a passable way, our institutions and our environment make us inclined to either shirk our democratic duty or to do a poor job at it, even when the stakes are high. They encourage us to focus on ourselves and our individual concerns rather than our collective well-being. Indeed, they also often make attempts at the political engagement necessary for working towards good political decisions more difficult thanks to the speed, volume, complexity, and incentives to manipulate others to get what you want that they encourage and enable.

...

Is democracy to blame for bad political decisions? In one sense, yes, at least partly. We elect representatives who make decisions on our behalf. We also come up with opinions and preferences that we communicate to them and to one another. Later, our leaders make decisions that are meant to reflect what we said we wanted. If they do not, well, it was our job to elect officials who would deliver the goods. If we fail to do so, if we elect—or fail to replace—officials who make decisions that produce poor outcomes, or if we hold preferences or opinions that support poor outcomes, then you might say that the democratic process is to blame. To say democracy is partly to blame is to say that our democratic institutions and other structures and systems that support them are only as strong as the quality of our participation.

In another sense, asking if democracy is to blame for bad political decisions is the same as asking if better decisions would be made under another system. We cannot know for sure. We cannot run an experiment in which we produce another world like our own, substituting a different form of government for ours, and check it against what we had. We might, however, look at non-democratic countries or our own non-democratic pasts and ask if, on balance, they produced better decisions and outcomes.

Well, it turns out that political scientists have done this. And it turns out that, on balance, democratic countries produce *far better* outcomes. They are generally more prosperous, more inclusive, more responsive, and more peaceful. Having citizens in charge of the political agenda—or, at least, permitting them to punish or reward politicians who deliver the results—produces better outcomes than in non-democratic states where the people have no regular recourse to hold politicians accountable and where, typically, human rights are severely limited.

But better does not mean perfect—or even adequate. "We do better than autocracies" is not exactly an inspiring slogan. Plus, there is no question that some political decisions produced by democracies have proven to be misguided, disastrous, unjust, or plainly evil. Canada has a reputation for being a kind, welcoming state, a multicultural mosaic of cultures and identities. That reputation, which deserves to be challenged even today, was inconceivable just decades ago. During the Second World War, Canada, a democracy, interned its own citizens of Japanese descent and turned away Jewish refugees fleeing oppression, violence, and death in Europe.

In May 1939, over nine hundred Jewish refugees left Hamburg to sail on the *St. Louis*, escaping Nazi Germany in search of safety. They were denied entry to several countries before setting off for Canada. Prime Minister William Lyon Mackenzie King, fearing a public backlash or even riots, responded by denying that the refugees were Canada's problem. King's approach reflected the Canadian anti-Semitism and xenophobia of the day, captured by the words of an anonymous immigration official who when asked how many Jewish refugees Canada should accept infamously replied, "None is too many." The *St. Louis* returned to Europe, where many on board were killed in the Holocaust. Between 1933 and 1945, Canada admitted a mere five thousand European Jewish refugees.

The 1940s also bore witness to Canada's hysterical response to the war against Japan, especially in the aftermath of the attack on Pearl Harbor. Beginning in 1942, the government rounded up over twenty-two thousand Japanese Canadians, most in British Columbia and most of whom were born in Canada, liquidating their property and confiscating the proceeds, and pressed many of them into work in internment camps in the West.

These events, xenophobic and racist, were not first offences for Canada, whose legacy of racist policies and actions include the Chinese head tax and the turning away of the *Komagata Maru*, a Japanese ship filled with South Asian immigrants that was refused entry at the Port of Vancouver in 1914. In recent years, anti-Muslim bigotry (especially in Quebec) and a racially charged national debate over the Syrian refugee crisis reminds us that the word *democracy* is not synonymous with the word *good*.

Democracies allow citizens to make political decisions, but that does not guarantee that those decisions will be good or just, or that the outcome of all those choices will support the survival of democracy, or even the survival of the species. The rise of nationalist populism in recent years has coincided with a decline in trust in democracy and its elected officials. Brexit, the rise of the alt-right, the culture wars, Trump. These are not accidents. They are the result of systemic bad decision-making arising from citizens' prejudice, hatred, apathy, alienation, and fear. All too often, and we are certainly seeing it now, a nasty feedback loop emerges. It makes it tougher for us to make good political decisions to counteract the bad ones that came before. Worse yet, it makes it easier for us to continue to make bad ones.

Now, this cycle is emerging at the worst time. The history of bad political decision-making has also been the history of social and political collapse. The stakes are high. Threats such as climate change, nuclear proliferation, mass war, epidemics, poverty and inequality, and even slavery—which, contrary to what many think, remains a serious global issue—loom large, already making life for millions precarious and miserable.

Democracies ask a lot of their citizens when they ask them to make political decisions—and even more when they ask for *good decisions*. Throughout most of human history, citizens were not asked or permitted to make political decisions. The few times it was tried, the political systems that emerged did not last long and were soon replaced by non-democratic forms of government in which leaders and elites did the thinking for their citizens. Over time, we reclaimed democratic government. But we should not imagine that just because we have regained it, we will not lose it again. Nor should we imagine that the decisions we produce will ensure human survival just because we produce them within the borders of a democratic country.

Democracy provides a system of government in which *we can* make good political decisions. Both of those italicized words are important: *we* (the people) *can* (are empowered to) make good political decisions. But it is on us to do so. Today, the need for good political decisions is at a high point as old challenges to living together meet new ones, and each is amplified by the speed and scale of the twenty-first century. It is

critically important that most of us make the necessary moral and intellectual progress—not just the scientific progress—to produce the sorts
of decisions that will help ensure that democracy survives, and we survive
along with it.

3. What is a good political decision?

"A good political decision is any decision I like." Tempting, right? There is a certain allure to simply defining a "good decision" in relation to its outcome and, more specifically, to whether you like that outcome. That's a fair impulse since, at a general level, this approach tends to work well enough. I bet most people would agree that good decisions should make people wealthier and healthier. And you would not get much pushback if you claimed that good decisions ensure that the species does not collapse. But how do we get that done? There is only so much time, attention, money, and human and natural resources to go around, and we disagree about how we should divide them. Moreover, we regularly disagree over what the good life should look like in practice, and we routinely debate what is right, true, correct, or beautiful. So even when we tend to agree on the easy, top-level stuff, such as health, wealth, and survival, we very quickly disagree on what this entails and how we should go about securing or distributing the benefits. Given that, the best chance we have on agreeing over what counts as a good political decision must be found elsewhere.

Recall what I said earlier. When I talk about a "good" political decision, I am referring to a *process* rather than an *outcome*. It is easy to see what a good political decision is if we look at the outcomes and choose the things we like, but that does not tell us much about the politics or decision-making that went into getting us to that outcome. If each of us could agree on how we should live together, how we should generate and distribute resources, or how we should go about settling disputes, then maybe we would find it easier to make decisions that would get us closer to that shared vision of the world. Good luck with that. So we need to think about good political decisions in a way that considers divided societies and persistent disagreement.

Enter: process.

Have you ever put together a piece of furniture? One day, you are sitting in a room in your home, looking around, and it comes to you: a shelf would really tie the room together! So off you go. In the showroom, the piece looks perfect. The colour will fit your room. The lighting brings it to life. The baubles placed on top of it make you feel like you are at home. "I'll take it!"

Now you are home with four large, heavy boxes, an instruction manual with exactly zero words and forty pictures, and Styrofoam packaging— everywhere. You have arrived at the critical moment: How am I going to put this thing together? What is my *process* going to look like? The temptation to toss the instructions is powerful. Out pops the devil on your left shoulder: he says, just figure it out on your own, this is crazy. After all, it is just a few pieces of lacquered wood, some dowels, and some screw nails. At that moment, out comes the angel on your right shoulder: he reminds you of the last time you tried to wing it, you know, with that "table" you put together. He reminds you of how long you spent mopping Thanksgiving dinner off the floor. Maybe the winging-it thing did not work out so well.

We need the angel on our right shoulder to enter our political decision-making. We need to override our desire to just make the easiest snap decisions—the ones that just *feel right* or merely reflect the way we have always done things.

Process matters. In some instances, when a group of people must decide on something, process may be the only thing that you can all agree on. And that is a start—an imperfect start that may lead to other issues down the road, but a start nonetheless. Agreeing on a process commits everyone to *accept* whatever outcome is reached, even if they do not *like* it. Without a good process, decisions will be driven by money, or influence, or even physical force. With a good process, you channel all the potential nastiness into a series of rules and norms that help manage disagreement.

At their best, elections do just that. Whether we like it or not, large and complex societies need to be governed. Since we disagree over who should govern and how, we need to come up with a set of rules and procedures to choose who will call the shots. In the past, rulers relied on hereditary arrangements or rule by whomever was strongest, but those forms of government rarely resulted in governments that governed for a broad range of their population. In many cases, times of instability or transition became violent and destructive. Democratic elections—free, fair, and routine—are a solution to managing disagreement about how we should live together. Everyone comes together to agree that every four or five years (sometimes more, sometimes less depending on the city, province/state, or country), according to a series of publicly known rules and procedures, candidates will present themselves to the people and try to win their votes. Those who fulfill the rules for being elected or forming government will win. They will then serve the people until they lose the next election, resign, are incapacitated or die, or are removed by a legal process. Through elections, we channel disagreement over substance into agreement over process so that we do not have to fight it out in the streets every time we must make a decision about what we should do.

But elections are imperfect mechanisms for good political decision-making, in part because of how we carry them out and the environment in which they are contested. Elections are infrequent affairs, even if they are routine. And the degree to which partisan bias, the force of money, and deliberate manipulation by strategic actors affect decisions is disconcerting. When you combine all of this with the speed at which elections are conducted, the volume of information citizens are asked to process in a short time, and the limited resources folks have to dedicate themselves to taking part in the contest, they fall far from their ideal of an informed electorate choosing the best candidates to represent them. But at least once you have a process that is agreed upon, you have something you can work with—you have the basis for doing better.

But what is a good political decision? Here is what I think makes one, if you will pardon some jargon that I will explain in a moment. A good political decision is based on a process of reasoning. During that process, a person should exercise their capacities for rationality and autonomy. If the individual has done this, we can reliably expect that they will come to the same or similar choices if they were asked to repeat the decision-making process. Additionally, they should be capable and willing to communicate their decision to others in a way that another reasonable person would be able to understand. And, most importantly, they must be able to *accurately* account for how and why they came to that decision, including awareness of their real motivations (rather than some rationalization).

I am talking here about good decisions in the context of being a citizen in a democracy—so, I am talking about decisions that are inherently *public* in a way that you deciding what to eat for dinner, what to study at university, or who to marry are not. But still, you may have political beliefs that are deeply personal. You may have burning commitments, and you are sticking to them. Most people have some issues on which they are never going to budge. So what is all this talk about process and reasons and changing your mind?

It turns out that on many issues, people are more flexible and reasonable than you would think—if you get the process right. Indeed, a good process can help not only change minds but bring about all kinds of other desirable outcomes. How? Part of the answer is trust. When people commit to a fair, inclusive process they generate trust. Good, trustworthy processes not only produce better outcomes—more rational, evidence based, easier to communicate to others—but those outcomes are more likely to be accepted by others (who are committed to and part of the process) as fair and legitimate, even if they do not agree with the outcome. And then we get more trust. It is a virtuous cycle.

There is lots of evidence that trust and good processes produce the sorts of things we want. Study after study and book after book teaches us that trust enables cooperation, helps drive economic growth, correlates with better health, encourages well-being, and protects against political dysfunction and the erosion of the norms and institutions that make democracy possible.[1]

None of that should come as a surprise. Trust is important to human life. It is part of who we are and how we live together; however, while it takes a lot of work to build trust, it is easy to lose it. So, we must work hard to get the process of political decision-making right if we want to reap the rewards it offers us. That requires us to bring people inside the system and to treat them with respect. We must also give them a chance to develop preferences through learning and deliberation, to be heard, and to see their desires reflected in policy and law. But before we can get to the *how* of making better decisions, we need to understand more about the internal workings of those good decisions and why you should care about making them.

Let's start with *rationality*. Here we have one of those concepts that drive scholars — political scientists, philosophers, economists — and all kinds of other folks mad. Rationality is one of those words that everyone is *pretty sure* they understand. But when you ask them to define it, they fumble around a bit and spit out something that makes good enough sense but may not jive with what the person beside them thinks it means. To make matters even more complicated, experts define rationality in different ways for different purposes — as a means-to-an-end efficiency, as a certain kind of wisdom, as the ability to reason or use logic, as the capacity to give reasons for doing things, and so on. I only mention the Silly Putty–like properties of the word because I am going to shape it in my own way to make my argument — that good political decisions require decision makers to be rational.

For the purposes of this book, I define *rationality* as the capacity to make sense of the world in a consistent, logical way that you can communicate to others. This definition assumes that individuals can consistently draw facts from the world, make sense of them by sorting and ordering them, and share them with others who can also make sense of them—even if they disagree. This definition includes the ability to learn *empirical* facts (stuff you can see, touch, hear, quantify, or understand by observation) and *normative* facts (assessments of how the world *should be* or about what is good based on reasoning, even though these will be more prone to disagreement than empirical facts).

A person who is behaving rationally will be able to go out the door, feel the cold air, see that the leaves have changed colour, notice some pumpkins on a neighbour's stoop, and conclude it is fall. They should also be able to explain to you why they support a policy by giving an account of the values or goods or outcomes that reflect it. I will come back to the word *reasons* a lot throughout this book. Being able to give reasons is critical to rationality, which is critical to making good political decisions.

Rationality is an important capacity because it allows us to make sense of the world; it unites us in the human endeavour of navigating complex, social existence on a planet that can be inhospitable to thinking. Now, reasonable people will use their rationality in ways that may lead them to disagree with others about empirical and normative facts, but when those disagreements include reasons that are stable and clearly communicated, they should at least make sense to others in a way that enables them to discuss and manage that disagreement.

We make sense of the world both individually and collectively. Rationality is publicly verified or, as some scholars put it, *validated*. How does that work? Well, rationality depends on what is known as an intersubjective process of validation. That is a technical way of saying that our ability to make sense of the world—to say that flower is yellow, that building is tall, that room is cold—is dependent on our ability to check that sense with other people.

Say you and I are out for a walk on a sunny day. We're in a park and stop to look at some flowers. I look down and point: "Isn't that a beautiful yellow flower?" In saying this, I am making sense of the world. I am seeing a thing that has certain properties. I call it a flower, and I describe one of those properties: its yellowness. You look at it and either affirm or challenge my view. "Yes! It's a beautiful yellow flower," or "What are you talking about? That's a beehive!" Over time and with enough validation by enough people, we take the raw world that is out there, filter it through our view and the views of others, and we start to name things, sort them, develop systems to study them, and agree on what these things are and how we should describe them.

Philosophy carries with it a long history of debate over how we know things. More specifically, thinkers in the philosophy of mind tradition have long asked how we gain knowledge through perception and share it with others. Debates stretch back at least to Aristotle, but things heated up in Europe in the seventeenth and eighteenth centuries when John Locke, Nicolas Malebranche, Gottfried Wilhelm Leibniz, David Hume, and George Berkeley sought to figure out what we take in through our senses and our minds, how we take it in, how we *know* we take it in, and how we can share what we take in with others to make sense of the world. Their debates stretched into the centuries that followed them, weaving in and out of other fields including psychology, neuroscience, and biology. In recent years, natural science has taken on a leading role in addressing questions of knowledge and perception, but philosophers still debate this stuff.

Whatever the philosophy or science says, most of the time enough of us agree on the basics of the physical world around us that we can live together coherently. But every so often, something comes along to remind us that perception varies from person to person. In 2015, an image of a dress went viral online and sparked a global debate that divided friends and families and strangers alike. The photograph that came to be known as The Dress is a picture of a lace dress by the designer Roman Originals. The photo looks normal enough—it's a dress. It's white and gold...or...well, no...Is it black and blue?

Viewers of the photo were divided on the colour of the dress, and for good reason: they were seeing it differently. As Adam Rogers wrote in *Wired* when he explained the science of why people disagreed on the colour: "This fight is about more than just social media—it's about primal biology and the way human eyes and brains have evolved to see color in a sunlit world."[2]

Once the controversy subsided, three sets of scientists published papers in *Current Biology* offering explanations of just how our biology sets us perceptually against one another.[3] The major takeaway from the studies is that colour can be tricky, especially depending on light conditions. Plus, our "internal models"—the guiding models our brain uses to interpret colour—are not always the same from person to person (and blue is a particularly tricky colour for us to process, especially in cases like The Dress, which was a poor-quality photo).

Much like we do with the perception of physical things, we also cobble together agreement about the normative world—the world of *should* instead of the world of *is*. Indeed, we regularly work with ethical and moral propositions that help us figure out how we want to live together. These moral and ethical propositions cannot be known the same way we can know facts about the physical world. But we can agree about what they mean. We can decide on whether they are acceptable, fair, or just. And we can adjust our lives accordingly. But all of that requires that we use reasons.

When it comes to politics, reasons are important. They are like currency that we exchange for outcomes, such as enacting a policy or convincing someone that your ideas are the right ones. In this conception of politics, reasons are central to both rationality (being able to understand the world and to communicate that understanding to others) and to political decision-making (I should have to give you reasons for or against the things I want or don't want us to do collectively).

We rely on reason giving in our day-to-day lives all the time. Let's say you and your partner wake up on a sunny Sunday and sit down to plan your day over breakfast. How do you think the day will go if you open with "So today we're hiking. Pack your things and I'll meet you in the car in twenty minutes!" I suspect you'll end up hiking alone—though I don't recommend testing this hypothesis. But what if, instead, you make your case: "It's so bright and warm out, we don't get many days like this, and I'd really like to get back in shape, which would be fun to do together. What do you think?"

In the first instance, you have asserted what is to be done, and in doing so you have turned the other person into a passive object to be directed towards your own ends. You have told them what is going to happen and ordered them to comply. Nobody enjoys being bossed around or treated like a mere passenger on the road trip of their own or someone else's life. In the second instance, however, by giving reasons and inviting a response, you have brought the other person into the conversation, giving them reasons and thus explaining to them why you would like to hike that day. The other person becomes an agent or a subject taking part in your collective endeavour of enjoying the day together. They can now respond to your reasons, accepting or rejecting them. They can even offer their own reasons, if they want to. Now, as co-agents, you can work out through exchanging reasons what you want to do with your day. That is certainly more pleasant than the first option, which runs you the risk of being met with the response: "Enjoy your hike. If you need me, I'll be at the beach."

Not everyone thinks of rationality and politics as an exercise in reason-giving. Some people practise rationality as a sort of clever skill for getting what you want however you can within the boundaries of the law, more or less. This is a sort of means-to-an-end approach to rationality, where reason is used to discover and achieve the most effective way to get from point A to point B and to get the desired outcome with the least pushback, regardless of how you treat others in the process.

Political campaigns are notorious for adopting this kind of ends-means rationality along with all the dubious strategies and tactics that accompany trying to win the race at nearly any cost. The 2016 Trump presidential campaign is a study in cynicism, replete with questionable behaviour, but one example stands out from a long list: the role of Cambridge Analytica in getting the Republican nominee elected.

It has been more than two years since Trump won the presidency, and reporting on the consulting firm that helped him reach the Oval Office is ongoing. In fact, we may never know all the details of precisely what went down. Cambridge Analytica itself has been wound up, and its former officials have gone on to work at a new data firm. But what we do know is that in 2016 the Trump campaign tapped the consultancy to help it build a digital operation on the strength of its promise to use digital methods — perhaps through big data, psychographics, and micro-targeting — to raise money and target voters. We also know that Steve Bannon, a former Trump adviser who joined the firm in 2016, convinced billionaire conservative donors Rebekah and Robert Mercer to fund the company, and facilitated a meeting between them and the Trump campaign. And finally, perhaps most jarring of all, we know that Cambridge Analytica got much of its data — as many as eighty-seven million Facebook profiles — from Aleksandr Kogan, a researcher who worked at the University of Cambridge, who had access to the information for other research purposes, and who sold it — against Facebook policy — to the company.

Critics point out that Cambridge Analytica's methods were flawed. They argue that the firm never delivered on its promise to use cutting-edge research in psychology and new techniques to persuade — or manipulate — voters into turning out for the Republican side. So maybe we are not deep into a techno hellscape of pervasive psychological manipulation at the highest levels — yet. But the trend is going that way, and it is being driven by technological advancements, unchecked ends-means rationality, and an obsession with winning at any cost.

Relying too much on this sort of rationality in politics is wrong, and it's a slippery slope towards really, really bad politics. Reason-giving based on good-faith, honest reasons for which the person can give an accurate account of their motivation for having them in the first place is a critical part of rational politics and good political decision-making. When people try to bypass deliberative rationality—the kind where we treat one another as citizens, as agents worthy of engagement and respect—and dive straight into manipulation or exploitation to get what they want, they undermine the democratic process. Compare that to when reasons are connected to deliberative rationality, when they form part of a process. When that happens, we get good political decisions, trust, and legitimate outcomes.

When some people hear the word *autonomy*, they assume it means the freedom to act independently. A country or a region is autonomous when it gets to run its own affairs. A person is autonomous when no one else is deciding how that person should act. But there is another way to think about the concept, one that can help us make better political decisions.

Let's start with a quick history lesson on the word itself. The word *autonomy* comes from the Ancient Greek words *autos* (self) and *nomos* (law). At some point, the word *autonomos* arose. It meant "having its own laws." Later, that word became *autonomia* and then, in the early seventeenth century, *autonomy*. In the eighteenth century, German philosopher Immanuel Kant dug into the concept. Kant was an interesting character: brilliant, diligent, sometimes boring, sometimes exciting and eccentric. He never ventured far from his village of Kønigsberg, in what was then Prussia and is now part of the Russian Federation. He never married. Legend has it that the villagers could set their watches by when he took his walk. But he was social and could hold his liquor with the best of them, even if it meant that he could not find his way home later in the evening.[4] Reading Kant, you quickly find yourself sympathizing with someone who cannot find their way home—the philosopher's books are dense. But they were revolutionary. Kant's ideas shaped modernity, and his thinking continues to influence people today, more than two hundred years after his death.

For Kant, the idea that autonomy is merely a synonym for freedom —or the absence of restraint—was insufficient. He distinguished between *autarchy* and *autonomy*. The first thing, autarchy, is the ability to make choices for yourself, whatever your motivations may be and whether or not you are aware of those motivations. You express autarchy if you get up off your couch, say, "I want some ice cream," and go to the store to get some.

The second capacity, *autonomy*, is more burdensome; it requires that you can rationally think about what you believe or want to do and give reasons for it. To meet the burdens of autonomy, it would not be enough to simply say, "I want some ice cream." You would have to give reasons why you want it. For instance, "I just saw an ad for Ben and Jerry's on TV, I am hungry, and I crave sugar."

There's our old friend rationality back again, firmly in place as the ultimate guarantor of sound, autonomous judgment. Kant's conception of autonomy requires that you do some work if you are to fulfill its requirements. It requires that you can reflect rationally on what you are doing and why you are doing it and can give *accurate* reasons for why you have come to whatever conclusion you happen to reach. Otherwise, you are acting *heteronymously*—that is, from more sources than just your own will (for instance, maybe you didn't notice the ice-cream ad because you were looking away, but suddenly, inexplicably, you want some Cherry Garcia).

What does autonomy look like in practice? Paul Sniderman is a distinguished political scientist who has spent much of his career learning about race, multiculturalism, and political decision-making in public life. In the 1980s, he and his colleagues in the United States studied Americans' support for welfare payments to African Americans. Then, as now, there was a lot of prejudice and misinformation about social assistance, and they looked into them as part of a study of how the public reasons about policy.

At first, their results look encouraging. As they write in their introduction to the study, "Citizens do not choose sides on issues like busing or abortion whimsically." So far, so good. But then things take a turn. "They have reasons for their preferences—*certainly they can give reasons for them*."[5] I have added the emphasis here. Because there it is: the twist.

"Certainly they can give reasons for them." But how do they reach those reasons? What is the process? And are those reasons an accurate reflection of what is driving them to reach the conclusions they arrived at?

In the case of government assistance to African Americans, Sniderman and his colleagues found that for less-educated individuals, affect — emotion, essentially — drove their conclusions, not political ideology. It was about how they *felt*. For those who were better educated, *ideology* did the work. However, in both cases, the researchers found that the explanations that people were giving for their support or opposition to social assistance to African Americans was based on *rationalization* rather than reasoning. What the study subjects were doing was "reasoning" *backwards*. Those whose opinions were driven by affect would immediately reach a conclusion without really thinking about it, and then double back to fill in the middle bits based on how we expect people to think about political issues — by providing evidence, thinking critically, and so forth.

What about those subjects who used "cognition-driven policy reasoning" — that is to say, those who used thinking rather than feeling to reach conclusions? It turns out that they "reason backward" too, working back from their conclusion to reasons and an explanation. And while they are more likely to use thinking over feeling than those who had less education, they are still more often rationalizers than reasoners. So a lot of people use how they *feel* as a shortcut to reach policy opinions. Then, when they must, they work backwards to tell a story, to give reasons, to spin evidence to fit their initial conclusion. Most of the time, individuals are unaware that they are thinking this way.

Now we're back to autonomy — or, rather, a lack of autonomy. If good political decisions rely on rationality and autonomy, the findings offered by Sniderman and his colleagues are a reminder that bad political decisions are common.

Autonomy is what I call a *keystone capacity*. It is a huge part of what makes us human and an equally large part of what makes us capable of making good decisions. Other capacities depend upon it. Autonomy connects our will — the things we fundamentally want to think, do, and be—through rationality and self-awareness to reasons that help us explain and understand our preferences, judgments, and actions to ourselves and, importantly for democracy, to others.

Autonomy is also related to what it means to be free. To understand just how, bear with me as I go a bit deeper into some philosophy. John Christman is a philosopher and political scientist at Penn State University who has been studying autonomy and liberalism for years. He defines autonomy as a state in which "the influences and conditions that give rise to the desire [or preference, judgment, action, etc.] were factors that the agent approved of or did not resist, or would not have resisted had she attended to them, and that the judgment was or would have been made in a minimally rational, non-self-deceived matter."[6]

Okay, let's take a breath. What Christman is getting at is that for someone to be autonomous, they need to know *why* they believe what they believe, *why* they prefer what they prefer, and *why* they do what they do. Next, they must be *okay* with the causes of their beliefs, preferences, and actions. Finally, folks need to be able to come to conclusions about the causes of their behaviour in a rational way, without lying to themselves—which is tough to avoid but can be managed by adopting a process for making better decisions and examining your motivations for believing what you believe. All of that sounds like a lot, but it should be a lot. You are not acting autonomously if you are lying to yourself, if someone is manipulating you, or if you are manipulating yourself.

Asking folks to be autonomous is a tall order. So it is understandable if you are inclined to wonder, "Who cares?" or, "Why should we care if someone is manipulating us, or if we are manipulating ourselves?" or even: "What if we are fine with the results of our behaviour, even if we are manipulated in the process of acting?" These are all good questions. But I have answers to them.

For one, there is reason to argue with the claim that manipulation produces good results. But let's set that aside for now and assume that manipulation *can* produce good results. I call this the *rose by any other name* challenge. In *Romeo and Juliet*, Shakespeare writes, "A rose by any other name would smell as sweet." The Bard was getting at the idea that it does not matter what you call something, what matters is what the thing itself fundamentally is. In this case, I am borrowing the phrase to raise the question: Does it matter *how we get to something* or is it the outcome that counts? Could a good outcome by any other process smell as sweet? Well, I think it *does* matter, because autonomy matters.

Going back to basics, Christman reminds us that our democratic politics is based on autonomy. He writes, "the nature and value of political freedom is intimately connected with the presupposition that actions one is free to do flow from desires and values that are truly an expression of the 'self-government' of the agent."[7] What he means is that our ideas about freedom, democracy, and the way we live together are based on a belief that what we want and what we think is important are products of our ability to *think for ourselves*. When that ability is taken away, we are no longer agents or subjects or citizens—we become the tool of others or of some shadowy force. We become *objects*.

No one is *completely* autonomous, of course. As much as some of us might like to imagine that we exist as we do independent of others or the world around us, that is simply not the case. Each of us is born into a time and place, and we are shaped by them, just as we are shaped by our family, friends, socio-economic class, education system, and even our bodies. The world around and inside us cuts broad paths for us to follow, at once enabling and constraining us, whether we like it or not. We cannot choose to live in a neutral environment with neutral bodies and neutral psychologies. We cannot access a world in which we simply sit down and decide entirely for ourselves, alone, what we ought to do.

We practise autonomy in relation to others, both in our day-to-day lives and when we make big decisions, like how to organize societies and states. Jennifer Nedelsky, a political and legal scholar at the University of Toronto, has written a lot on the idea of relational autonomy. "What makes autonomy possible is not being independent of all others, but constructive relationships—with parents, teachers, friends, colleagues and officials of the state. Autonomy is thus also not a characteristic that we simply achieve," she writes. "Its flourishing depends on the kinds of relationships...of which we are a part." She lists "biases, fears, emotions that cloud rather than facilitate judgment" as challenges that emerge from a focus on "private considerations."[8] Autonomy is critical to good political decisions, but none of us is an island. To make good political decisions, we must develop and use our ability to think and reason autonomously, but we should also keep in mind that this ability is bound up in our lives as social animals. We need each other to survive. Evolution has not adapted us to live alone—and it certainly has not adapted us to make decisions alone.

But let's get back to the question of how autonomy helps produce good outcomes. Above all, autonomy helps ensure that you or some group you are part of is not dominated by others for their own interests. Right there, autonomy is worth the price of admission. Our democratic political system has been built to ensure that individual citizens remain autonomous, that they have the freedom to decide for themselves how to live their lives if we use it properly.

But there is something even more fundamental at work with autonomy. We believe that there is an inherent value to self-determination—to deciding how you want to live based on your own terms. That self-determination requires autonomy. We have taken freedom and self-determination as organizing principles for our lives. When we fail to act autonomously, we are unfree, we are not self-determining. Because autonomy is a necessary condition for deciding what we want to do, when we want to do it, what goals we want to pursue, and how we want to live our lives.

...

So far in our quest to discover what a good political decision is we have covered rationality and autonomy. Good political decisions are based on facts and reasons that we can communicate to others. They are also based on a capacity to choose for ourselves what we want to do with self-awareness of *why* we think, believe, or act the way we do.

Rationality and autonomy are therefore essential to good political decision-making. But they aren't enough; good political decisions must also be *reliable*.

For all our flaws and shortcomings, we humans are decent at making sense of the world. In philosophy, a concept called naïve realism holds that we perceive the world *as it is*—that our senses take in what is out there as it exists. But that is not what happens. When we perceive the world, when we see, touch, taste, hear, or feel what's out there, our brain doesn't *receive* the world as much as it *recreates* it in our heads.

Each human is a unique combination of genetic code and lived experience; none of us is alike. On top of that, the world "out there" is reproduced for each of us in a process in which our individuality frames and distorts it in ways that may vary and which we can never entirely perfectly verify. This is the stuff that keeps philosophers up at night. But we find a way to make life work anyway. We find a way to make sense of things.

But for the world to make sense collectively, we need that sense making to play out more or less the same way under similar conditions. That consistency is the foundation that allows us to accept that reliability in decision-making is possible. Of course, you might change your mind. The facts may change. Your values may change. You might learn something. You might forget something. All kinds of things might happen. But if the circumstances are the same, and you are the same, you should come up with the same decision—if you are making reliable decisions.

The problem with reliability is that small changes that should be irrelevant to your decision can have a profound effect on what you decide. It shouldn't matter which logically equivalent statement is used in an argument. But remember the 10 per cent failure rate and 90 per cent success rate? Those should be treated the same. However, we know from behavioural science research that people will make different decisions based on wording alone.[9]

Reliability is important for good decision-making because we're stuck with one another, and we need to cooperate. That cooperation requires reliability, since we cannot afford to waste time every day trying to figure out if the decisions we made yesterday still hold today. Reliable decisions help establish structure and build trust among individuals. They ground the world and make it predictable, which makes living together much easier, and frees up time to solve other problems, create art, explore the world, and enjoy the company of one another.

More broadly, the quest for reliability is related to the human need for security. It is hard to make good decisions—political or otherwise—from a position of insecurity. To be secure, we need something that the sociologists call ontological security. Prominent British thinker and sociologist Anthony Giddens defines ontological security as "Confidence or trust that the natural and social worlds are as they appear to be, including the basic existential parameters of self and social identity."[10] He means that ontological security exists when we can know and make sense of the world—both the physical world and our social (and political) relationships—in a consistent, predictable way and when we are confident others see it the same way.

Finally, good political decisions are shareable. If you were born after 1984, the word *shareable* might suggest social media and internet memes. That is okay, but when you see it here, I want you to think of shareable content as information that you can communicate to another and reasonably expect them to understand. Many of our political decisions require that we communicate with others in some way—voting, giving our opinions to a pollster or a politician, speaking up at a town hall, or debating with family and friends over dinner. This is what I'm calling the *principle of shareability*.

Here is how that principle works: we should be able to share our political decisions with others *by giving them reasons for those decisions*. And those reasons should be rationally and autonomously generated. Even better, we should be able to explain those reasons in ways that accurately represent our motivations for believing what we believe rather than just rationalizing our way out of the conversation, hiding from others—and perhaps ourselves—the truth of what we believe and why we believe it.

For instance, say there is a proposal on the table to build a highway that will cut through a neighbourhood.[11] The proposal requires that homes and businesses in a part of that community be torn down to make way for the highway. The new highway will irrevocably change how people in that community live and work. This sort of issue will undoubtedly be contentious, since it will pit those who live in the town against those who would benefit most from the highway without sacrifice. Furthermore, the debate is likely to involve some degree of battle over whether (or when) it is okay to do something that may benefit the many at great cost to the few. Here, reasons are particularly important. It is not enough for the government to say, "Hey, we want to build this highway, so pack your bags."

The reasons offered by the side in favour of building the highway will likely include the need to facilitate travel and the transportation of goods. Cities cannot grow, they will say, if they cannot branch outward, connecting to other towns and cities and building gateways to other provinces and states, and perhaps even countries. You may not agree with these reasons, and you may even reject the underlying premise upon which they rest—that development is necessary for social, political, and economic well-being and growth. Or you might not think that a new highway is the only or best way to achieve these ends. But reasonable people will at least be able to recognize these reasons *as reasons*. And that is fine. After all, reasons you disagree with or see as insufficient to warrant action are very different—and better from a democratic perspective—than no reasons at all.

For its part, the community that would be affected by the highway is likely to offer reasons that include the desire to preserve itself or the desire to avoid the significant, life-altering disruption that comes with highway building. It may even oppose development by offering reasons that push back against capitalism or major road projects (who says a highway is the only way to move people and goods? And who says either needs to move?). Once again, you may not agree with all or any of these reasons, but if you are acting as a good-faith citizen, you should be able to recognize them *as reasons*.

This hypothetical example is not so hypothetical. In fact, it is a micro-example consistent with one of the largest infrastructure projects in human history: the US interstate highway system.

In the 1950s, President Eisenhower supported a national highway plan that had been in the works in various forms for decades. Construction began in 1956, supported by federal funds. It was a planner's dream that would take decades and billions of dollars to build as the system stretched to nearly fifty thousand miles. And while the project faced opposition, and some sections of the highway were left unbuilt because of local resistance, the creation of the interstate system was not exactly a community-by-community deliberative endeavour.

As much as there were reasons for the interstate system—connecting the country, enabling goods and services to move, supporting national defence—it came at a cost. For instance, in a 1997 report by the Transit Cooperative Research Program, sponsored by the Federal Transit Administration, researchers argued that the interstate harmed public transit by making it less competitive—privileging highways, driving suburbanization, hollowing out cities, and eroding public transit capacity.[12] Where were the voices, decades ago, of those who needed to be heard? What did a lack of their input do to transportation patterns in America and, consequently, to communities within the city core? Recent American history has been, in part, the story of troubled cities and growing suburbs, driven in part by a federal project from over sixty years ago.

Of course, with particularly contentious political issues, there will always be a constituency that is upset and dissatisfied if its side doesn't prevail. But by offering reasons—rather than, say, buying someone off, immediately calling a vote, manipulating the group, threatening legal or even violent action, or just plain steamrolling the project through—you are recognizing those individuals as persons with real and valid preferences of their own. You are also creating a sort of currency in which everyone can participate by exchanging their reasons. This process increases trust, compliance, motivation to come back to the table in the future, and legitimacy. Even better, sometimes reasons convince others to change their minds. Each of these is a democratic good enabled by reasons that you can communicate to others whom you recognize as fellow participants in decision-making—participants worthy of recognition, respect, and inclusion.

I have been banging on a lot about what makes a good political decision —and I have talked a little bit about why good political decisions are themselves, well, *good*. But wait! There's more! Five more reasons why you should care about good political decisions, that is.

First, good political decisions produce more rational outcomes. In 2017, I completed a PhD in political science. During my doctoral research years, I had a supervisor, Mark E. Warren, who taught me a lot about deliberative democracy, the sort of democracy I have been discussing in this book. One of his insights is that, these days, our politics cannot just rest on appeals to "the nation" or patriotism or the commandments of a strong political or religious leader. He argues that the legitimacy of our political decisions rests on *rational legitimacy*, meaning that it comes from a process in which we get together, give one another reasons for what we want to do—or not do—and produce "motivational force."[13] In other words, these decisions give you a basis to respect and follow them, since they are backed by reasons rather than, say, some justification like "Because I said so" or "This is how we've always done things."

The sorts of good political decisions I've been talking about so far fit with another idea Mark used to talk about: good political decisions rely on us coming together to express what we want to do and why we want to do it. That's the *rational* bit. The decisions we reach and the actions we take are the result of us working out our issues among ourselves, justifying to one another with reasons why this or that or the other thing matters. And the payoff is huge: more rational decisions are better at matching outcomes to what people really want.

Second, good political decisions generate more ethical and inclusive outcomes. The process of good political decision-making that I discuss in this book has an ethical function based on treating individuals as an end in themselves rather than as a means to an end. That is why it is important that decisions are rational and autonomous, since these sorts of decisions tend to reflect a more rigorous assessment of the world around us and an honest account of our motivations for voting one way or another, or for holding this or that political opinion. Good political decisions therefore *include others*, directly or indirectly. This inclusion reflects a commitment to what is known in political science as the *all-affected-interests principle*—the idea that all of those affected by some decision ought to be included in some way in making it.

The ethical function of good political decisions helps smooth over the challenges that we face because we are stuck together and often stuck disagreeing. When you commit to making rational, autonomous, reliable, and shareable decisions, you commit to including others, to respecting them as free human beings, and to treating them respectfully rather than as an object you can use to achieve your ends—or an impediment to you reaching those ends.

Third, good political decisions are more legitimate. They reflect our true motivations and they give us a better sense of who we are and what we want. When it comes to *others*, good political decisions, since they are inclusive and perceived as fair, produce outcomes that others will accept. These sorts of decisions encourage buy-in, even from those who do not get their way.

Fourth, good political decisions help build trust. Trust is essential to democracy. Without trust, it is hard to get things done. Relationships built around strategic interests—where one or more parties try to get something from the others—are trust minefields. Our politics are chock full of strategic relationships. In moderation, that is fine. In fact, you cannot do politics—or much at all—without these kinds of relationships. But they are susceptible to all kinds of bad behaviour, such as when a legislator in the United States adds an unrelated item to a bill to secure the votes needed for it to pass (and politics becomes strategic horse trading). And when interests change, strategic relationships fray and break apart.

Trust requires that, over time, individuals and groups see one another as consistent and honest actors. The folk wisdom that trust is difficult to gain but easy to lose is true. Once trust is broken, a weak spot in the relationship emerges. If that weak spot takes a hit in the future, it is even more susceptible to collapsing. Good political decisions encourage trust by leveraging the other good bits I have been talking about so far: the rational, ethical, inclusive, legitimate bits. By doing the hard work of collecting information about the world, critically thinking it through, communicating it to others honestly, offering reasons for your conclusions and consequent preferences, and respecting others who do the same, you are creating good conditions for trust building. Not everyone will trust everyone else, not everyone will get what they want all the time. But good political decisions create the conditions for trust, which in turn help support an environment in which you can make good political decisions—a virtuous cycle.

Finally, I return to self-determination. For hundreds of years we have been living our lives backstopped by the idea that we should be able to decide how we want to live, individually and collectively. This idea encourages us to respect ourselves as rational, independent decision makers—subjects, not objects—and, at its best, it encourages us to think of others in the same way. It also encourages us to reflect upon how we want to shape our world.

But countless times we have gone ahead and screwed it all up. We have made messes time after time — little ones, big ones, and very big ones. But our failures are not caused by the ideal of self-determination; they are caused by our failure to organize and decide in a way that commits us to linking self-determination to a process of decision-making designed to produce rational, ethical, inclusive, trust-building, and legitimate outcomes, and by our failure to then commit to building individual and institutional capacity to support that endeavour. Today, we need to commit to such a process — not just to live better lives but to improve the chances that the next generation will be around to live any sort of life at all.

TWO

Why do we make bad political decisions?

4. Our bodies, our minds, mental shortcuts, and the media

We make bad political decisions because we live in a world that is often inhospitable to rational, autonomous judgment, and we have evolved in such a way that it is hard for us to avoid falling into traps that encourage us to get it wrong. Far too often, making a good political decision with the mental equipment we have and the environment in which we live is like trying to drive a Lamborghini up a snowy mountain trail: the tool isn't fit for the task.

That is the bad news: when it comes to political decision-making, we are not "designed" for the job, and the world we live in does not make things any easier on us. And when I say "us" I mean *all of us*. We all make bad political decisions. You do. I do. Your neighbour does. Your family members do. Lawyers and doctors do. Presidents and prime ministers do. There's no person alive, nor has there ever been, who has not made a bad political decision or two.

It may seem strange that we routinely make bad political decisions. After all, we as a species have been at it for a long time. Why haven't we figured it out by now? Well, there are a few related factors that run deep. One of them, I am afraid to say, is us: our biology and our psychology are fickle friends — or frenemies — to good political decision-making. Now, a few caveats are in order on this one. Neither our biology nor our psychology is, on its own, fully determinative of who we are or what we do. Sure, our bodies and our brains place limits on us, and they make certain sorts of behaviour more or less likely or easier or harder to accomplish. But we are not hard-wired to fail at making good political decisions.

Our biology and our psychology are intertwined. Our brain is *part of our body* and our minds are a product of our bodies existing in the world. And while we cannot separate mind and body, we can sort biology from psychology for the purposes of evaluating different processes and behavioural phenomena. So with biology, I will be referring to human beings as a carbon-based species made up of blood and guts and bones, sharing some similarities with other species in the animal kingdom. With psychology, I will be referring exclusively to processes of the mind, a function of our biology, of our bodies, something the body does that can be studied separately from other discussions of biology. But I will still talk about them together under the category of us, of the ways in which *we* are the problem.

Another reason we make bad political decisions is related to how we organize ourselves: our institutions make good political decision-making more difficult than it needs to be. In fact, in some cases, our institutions *encourage* bad political decisions and— surprise, surprise—bring about bad outcomes.

Remember, we need institutions. And for the most part, our institutions do a lot of good work. But they can be a part of the problem. Think of partisan politics, electoral systems, political campaigns, the media, the education system, political ideology, the free market, and even liberal democracy itself. They produce good outcomes, but they can also make a mess because they contribute to bad political decision-making. If we want to do better, we must consider ways that we can change them.

A third reason we make bad political decisions is that our milieu—our broader environment and the conditions under which we live together—is set up in a way that makes good political decision-making difficult. Left unchecked, the speedy, complicated, information-heavy world around us can work against us.

...

Try to get outside your body for a moment. Just pop out of your corporeal vessel and meet me across the room. You cannot, of course. Try as you might, you are your body, and you are stuck with it. We have a long history of trying to get unstuck, though — of trying to separate the body and the mind.

The most famous proponent of what is known as mind-body dualism, roughly the idea that body and mind are separate things, is René Descartes, a French philosopher who lived in the seventeenth century. Descartes believed that the body is a kind of machine that houses the mind, which itself is nothing like a machine but rather a nonmaterial substance that interacts with the body to produce human beings (through the pineal gland, which exists but does not, it turns out, do what Descartes thought it did) and, moreover, to *control* them. We now know that Descartes was mistaken and that mind is *something the body does* in relation to the environment in which it exists.[1] Notice that I say *the body* and not just *the brain*, since psychology is affected by far more of our corporeal form than just the bit at the top.

Also, far from being state-of-the-art machines for navigating the information age, our bodies are quite old. Well, evolutionarily speaking, anyway. They have been shaped by natural selection in such a way that the minds they produce have some behavioural tendencies that run up against what many of us desire and expect from ourselves, even if some adaptations have been helpful.

When we walk around in our bodies, we carry with us the legacy of millions of years of evolution. As much as we might imagine ourselves as rational masters of the universe, that conception is upset by the reality that we are just fancy primates. And our nature shapes and directs our behaviour, even if it does not fully determine how each one of us will behave in every instance.

If you have paid any attention to our species, you might have noticed that there are a few things we tend to value and a few ways we tend to behave. We like sex a lot. We are violent — often. And we eat food *all the time.* In *Enlightenment 2.0,* University of Toronto philosopher Joseph Heath imagines human memory as an old "closed stacks" library staffed by a slightly unhelpful librarian with "an unhealthy preoccupation with sex, violence, and food."[2] He's right. Of course, we often control our drives to reproduce, fight for resources and space, and eat, but they remain influential—and sometimes they override our rational preferences and goals. So on the journey to good political decision-making, we start off a bit lost.

You cannot separate the mind and the body, but let's pretend for a second that you can so that we can talk about our mind on its own. The first thing we must do is recognize that we are inherently of *two minds.* More precisely, we are of *two sorts of psychological processing,* which affects how we understand the world. In psychology, this phenomenon is known as the dual-process model. In it, reasoning is divided into two sorts, most famously expounded by the Nobel Prize-winning psychologist Daniel Kahneman. In his book *Thinking, Fast and Slow,* Kahneman divides reasoning into two systems: System 1 and System 2. Now, these systems are *metaphors.* There is no System 1 or System 2 area of the brain, nothing you can point to and say, "Aha! I see it." These two systems are simply groupings of attributes that explain different processes for thinking about and responding to stuff that happens in the world.

Kahneman summarizes the two systems with some useful shorthand. System 1 is the gut-based driver of behaviour; it "operates automatically and quickly, with little or no effort and no sense of voluntary control." When I ask, "Is it wrong to kill humans for sport?" I immediately answer that it is, without thinking about it, just as when I say, "Think of a cute kitten," an image of an adorable little cat comes to mind. You cannot help it. System 1 works by intuition and association, with little or no reflection; Kahneman calls it "the associative machine."

System 2, on the other hand, is what Kahneman calls the "lazy controller." Its primary job is to "monitor and control thoughts 'suggested' by System 1." It does the "mental work." According to Kahneman, System 2 "allocates attention to the effortful mental activities that demand it, including complex computations. The operations of System 2 are often associated with the subjective experience of agency, choice, and concentration." But System 2 is often overwhelmed and easily tired. Using it is resource intensive and, unfortunately, inefficient—especially compared to System 1, which breezes along effortlessly. So we tend to allocate limited resources to paying attention to the world. Consequently, we miss quite a bit. Remember the person in the gorilla suit in that experiment earlier? Nonetheless, when we think of *ourselves* and *who we are*, we tend to think in terms of System 2, "the conscious, reasoning self that has beliefs, makes choices, and decides what to think about and what to do." And we set our expectations accordingly.[3]

Dual-process models help explain how human beings operate in an environment for which we did not specifically evolve. We changed over millions of years to be eminently suited for a hunter-gatherer life: more compact, simpler, nature-based, and in smaller communities. We needed to be able to make snap decisions about imminent danger, to be able to constantly scan our environs and discard what was not deemed dangerous, remaining ever alert. System 1 evolved for that. System 2's sober second thought was important, too, though. It let us learn to craft tools and tame fire, to figure out the things that would give us an edge, since our relatively slow, bipedal bodies otherwise made us easy prey. Together the two systems made us formidable. But how these two systems work together is not always so useful in the world we now inhabit.

Obviously, that does not mean that we should not or cannot live in large, complex, demanding, pluralist, multicultural, and multi-ethnic societies. But it does mean that we will experience some serious glitches in the process, and those might cause us some trouble. Dual-process theory bridges biology and psychology, linking our past and our present. Lucky for us, it also sheds some light on how we might improve our future. Because it turns out that System 1 is not just responsible for me getting you to think about kittens and reminding you that hunting humans for sport isn't okay: it also plays an active, regular role in our politics, our morality, and even in how we conceive of the world.

So how do System 1 and System 2 muck up the waters of rational, autonomous decision-making? Well, in lots of ways. But a few stand out — particularly framing, priming, agenda-setting, and heuristics. These are known as media effects.

Before we get to them, a quick caveat: media effects remind me of philosopher Thomas Nagel's claim that there is no such thing as a "view from nowhere" — you cannot get outside yourself, look down upon the world, and evaluate things from above. Like it or not, you are always in the thick of it. The same is true for political decision-making and the news. Unless you attend every speech and press conference, unless you head to the legislature in person, unless you visit politicians and experts and civil society practitioners one by one, you are going to have to get most of your information from the news media — and, consequently, you will be exposed to agenda-setting, priming, and framing effects. So, there is no getting away from them. But as we become better political decision makers, we can know what to look for and better manage these effects. So there we are starting off on an encouraging note.

Framing

Let's begin with framing. I could fill a barn with the books and articles written on what is known as the framing effect. Simply put, the framing effect occurs when the way something is presented (for instance, how it is worded) affects how a person responds to it. Since politics depends on communication and requires us to make all kinds of decisions in a competitive environment filled with different messages, you can see why framing matters quite a bit.

Here is how the effect works. Imagine you are asked to decide what to do about an expected outbreak of an uncommon, mysterious disease. This is the problem that Daniel Kahneman and Amos Tversky put to subjects in a famous experiment published in a 1981 paper called "The Framing of Decisions and the Psychology of Choice."[4] They put the scenario to folks like this: "Imagine that the US is preparing for the outbreak of an unusual Asian disease, which is expected to kill 600 people. Two alternative programs to combat the disease have been proposed." The authors separated the subjects of the study into two groups and gave each a set of two options for dealing with the outbreak. Both sets of selections were identical, but they were worded differently, to emphasize gains or losses. The first group was given these options (the percentage who chose A or B is listed in square brackets, just as Kahneman and Tversky presented their findings in 1981, though participants did not see these numbers while they took part):

> If Program A is adopted, 200 people will be saved. [72 per cent]
> If Program B is adopted, there is 1/3 probability that 600 people will be saved, and 2/3 probability that nobody will be saved. [28 per cent]
> Which of the two programs would you favor?

You will notice that a huge majority of folks opted for Program A, in which two hundred people are saved, but in which four hundred people are *not saved* and therefore die. They chose the simpler and less risky of the two options—preferring a bird in the hand to two in the bush. Here are the options presented to the second group of participants.

> If Program C is adopted 400 people will die. [22 per cent]
> If Program D is adopted there is 1/3 probability that nobody will die, and 2/3 probability that 600 people will die. [78 per cent]
> Which of the two programs would you favor?

Suddenly, in the second set of programs, everyone is a risk taker! Once Program A is reframed to emphasize *loss* instead of *gain*, people become more risk seeking, rolling the dice on the lives of hundreds of people. As Kahneman and Tversky put it: "choices involving gains are often risk averse, and choices involving losses are often risk taking." When situations are different, that can make sense, but when they are logically the same, we have a problem.

Political decisions are subject to framing effects like any other sort of decision, but the nature of politics encourages deliberate manipulation to an extent matched by few other issue areas. Above, the sort of framing I discussed is known as *equivalency framing*—the same message can be formed in different but equivalent ways. In the social sciences, framing sometimes takes on a different definition than the one I have offered above—known as *emphasis framing*. With emphasis framing, the choice of wording involves considerations such as what to name something ("the death tax" for estate taxes), what to emphasize in a story (say, race or gender or social class), and what sort of adjectives, images, or values to use when describing an issue or options ("hard-working," "family," "social justice").

Now, admittedly, everybody frames. You frame, I frame, the media frames, corporations frame, politicians frame. Not everyone frames deliberately or strategically. But everybody frames. With political issues, framing is often employed as a strategic tool to win rather than to develop understanding or to reach the most rational or acceptable outcome. Framing can be used to help make issues accessible to people, but it's often used to mislead or manipulate citizens, encouraging them to make decisions they otherwise would not have made. In other words, framing is often used to work against rational, autonomous decisions—against what I have been calling good political decisions.

One of my favourite examples of framing at work is the naming of bills, acts, and political projects. As we go, keep in mind the idea that *naming is framing*. Pay close attention to the names used and what they call to mind. Try to imagine what sort of reactions—thoughts, connotations, feelings—a different name for the same bill or act might conjure up. Ask yourself whether the name persuades you to support or oppose the bill or act, whether it makes you want to learn more about it or to ignore it.

Perhaps the most (in)famous example of emphasis framing in North American politics is the one I just mentioned: the "death tax." The name is evocative, that's for sure. You are born, you work all your life, you pay your fair share, and then you die—and the government *still taxes you!* *Right to the bitter end!* I mean, what kind of government taxes someone *for dying?* That is how opponents of the US federal estate tax want you to think about the issue—and have since the 1940s.[5] This sort of framing encourages people to consider the measure as a tax on death, rather than on the estates or inheritances, which is what is taxed when a person dies.

Let me give you some more examples. In 2017, an American Republican lawmaker proposed the World's Greatest Healthcare Plan of 2017 to replace President Obama's Affordable Care Act. The same year, a Democrat in the House of Representatives introduced the COVFEFE Act to protect the US president's social media records—named after a bizarre tweet of Donald Trump's, sent late at night, which read: "Despite the constant negative press covfefe." Of course, President Trump himself knows how to play the framing game, suggesting a "catchy" name for his party's tax plan: the Cut, Cut, Cut Bill. And then there was DOMA, the Defense of Marriage Act, which, before being ruled unconstitutional, defined marriage as being between a man and a woman. It was discriminatory against same sex couples but was framed as a "defense" of marriage.

Then there is the USA Patriot Act, set up in the aftermath of 9/11. It is not quite what it sounds; it is actually an acronym: Uniting and Strengthening America by PATRIOT (Providing Appropriate Tools Required to Intercept and Obstruct Terrorism). Congress loves its framing acronyms. In 2013, for instance, 240 bills were acronyms, including BREATHE (Bringing Reductions to Energy's Airborne Toxic Health Effects), CHURCH (Congressional Hope for Uniform Recognition of

Christian Heritage), Opportunity KNOCKS (Opportunity Kindling New Options for Career and Knowledge Seekers), and TRAUMA (Trauma Relief Access for University Medical Assistance).

There have been a few framing gems in Canada, too. In 2010, the Conservative government passed the Cracking Down on Crooked Consultants Act, which amended the Immigration and Refugee Protection Act to protect new arrivals to Canada from scammers. In 2015, the same government offered the Zero Tolerance for Barbaric Cultural Practices Act—a move that many deemed racist and helped the Conservatives lose the federal election later that year. There has also been a Red Tape Reduction Act, a Respect for Communities Act, and a Fair Elections Act (which was criticized by many for making elections less fair).

But is framing always an exercise in misleading or manipulating people by strategically emphasizing certain things and not others? Can framing be good? How does it affect citizen competence? The American political scientist James N. Druckman has dug into these questions in search of the good, the bad, and the ugly effects of framing. He looked into just how good citizens are at processing and acting on such information, especially in light of attempts by elites to manipulate them. He assessed the research on framing and found that a lot of what we might think of as citizens changing their perspective because of framing is them changing their mind because they have learned new information or come across a new consideration. His research suggests that we have some reasons to be concerned, but overall we should not worry.

Despite his reassurances, I do worry.

Ask yourself the following question: What does it mean to be a citizen? What does that role entail? Druckman reminds us that "a basic conception of democratic competence...requires that citizens be well qualified or capable to meet their assigned role."[6] Being a competent citizen means doing your job as a citizen well. And what is that job? Druckman draws on a long history of political science and philosophy to suggest that the role is "the expression of [your] preferences to which governors can and should respond." We elect representatives to, well, represent us. To do so, we need to be able to communicate our preferences to them so that in the long run they can make the sort of policies and pass the sort of laws that we want. Here we get to the tricky part. Druckman concludes, "Thus, competent citizens must be 'capable' of forming preferences." (In this case, *competent* means that citizens should not be manipulated by elites and their preferences should not be arbitrary.)

But how does framing affect how we form preferences? When politicians or other elites use frames like a "just war" or "This campaign is about the economy!" frequently, they make those frames familiar and more accessible in the mind of citizens. The effect is not universal or automatic, but it occurs often enough to raise concerns about manipulation. Your political decision is neither rational nor autonomous if it is merely the product of conditioning based on the repetition of a catchy frame (remember the "death tax"?).

To adapt another example from Druckman, consider this: would you prefer a policy that produced 90 per cent employment or one that resulted in 10 per cent unemployment? The first policy sounds more appealing, right? Who wants 10 per cent unemployment? The two statistics are implying the same thing, of course. But framing matters.[7]

In a world in which there's someone to point out that the above example of 90 per cent employment/10 per cent unemployment amount to the same thing, equivalency framing effects have much less power. However, in a politically polarized environment in which people are increasingly getting their news from "sources they trust" — that is, sources that play to their pre-existing beliefs and biases — framing effects are particularly pernicious. Framing effects can therefore be used by politicians and other interested groups or individuals to play to our cognitive predispositions, to exploit our biases, and to encourage us to make decisions we wouldn't otherwise make or else would make differently — that is, bad political decisions.

Agenda-setting

How do we know what to pay attention to? In a world of limited time, amid our busy lives, how do we decide which political issues are important to us and which we will ignore? Most of us are not deeply involved in the political world day to day. So how do we sort through the countless issues, characters, events, and controversies that inform it?

For many, the answer is the media. In a world where time is a scarce resource, someone must be the gatekeeper—letting in what is essential and keeping out the distracting, unnecessary bits. When the media signals to people what they should think about based on what they, the media, choose to cover, when they choose to cover it, and in what order, it is known as *agenda-setting*.[8] Agenda-setting is important because those who control the agenda of the day are central to deciding which issues will make up our political world. Perhaps the leading scholar of media effects in politics, American political scientist Shanto Iyengar, notes that the media motivates politicians to act on certain issues based on whether, and how, they are covered.[9] But politicians can also affect what the media covers. It is a symbiotic relationship—or parasitic, depending on your perspective. Citizens can affect media coverage and political activity, too, but how do they know *what to care about in the first place?* For the most part, they know because someone in the media or another trusted source like an advocacy organization or faith group has picked up on the issue and told them about it.

Is this good or bad news for political decision-making? Well, it depends. As I mentioned, we rarely have time to go to the original source of the issue and figure out for ourselves what's going on in the political world, so we let the media do that work for us. We divide the labour and let them specialize. But here is where we get into trouble. The psychological mechanism behind agenda-setting is *availability*.[10] It seems that agenda-setting is driven by what are known as "top-of-head" considerations, easily accessed because they are *available* to us. And the stuff that is available to us is not always representative of what is most important.

To the extent that we trust the media to act responsibly as gatekeepers, as trustees of the sacred political agenda, we ought not to worry too much, right? The media is made up of all sorts, including many journalists beyond reproach who do the difficult work of digging and sorting, work that we simply cannot do on our own. They are hard-working folks, and the work they do is essential. However, journalists make mistakes, local news is dying, corporate consolidation of the media is on the rise, and partisan media (in the United States, Canada, and elsewhere) are driving political polarization. Importantly, issues that ought to be covered get ignored or left behind in the twenty-four-hour news cycle that somehow seems increasingly vapid despite having more time to cover the news than ever before (though not necessarily the personnel to do so).

In the spring of 2018, *Vox* looked at Fox News—America's most-watched cable news network—and compared its news coverage to CNN and MSNBC.[11] It found that Fox, a conservative outlet, spent considerably less time than mainstream media covering the Mueller investigation into Donald Trump's presidential campaign and Russian interference in the 2016 election, the Puerto Rico hurricane, health care, Environmental Protection Agency director Scott Pruitt and his imbroglios, and other significant national news stories. They also found that Fox spent *more* time covering mainstream media and "fake news," Hillary Clinton, the Mexican border, national-anthem kneeling, and gun rights.

As Alvin Chang, the writer of the piece, put it: "The best way to think of Fox News is that it's an identity-reinforcing machine." And while supporters of Fox News might say the same thing about CNN and MSNBC (somewhat unfairly), that also reflects the point that outlets are seen by folks, accurately or not, as partisan. Viewers then self-select accordingly, shutting themselves off from alternative views, constructing echo chambers and locking themselves snugly inside. This partisan ensconcing reinforces incentives for outlets like Fox to give people the content and spin they want, regardless of whether it is accurate or representative of what is out there in the world, or how important a story or issue might be relative to others.

And what is worse, social media reinforces and extends the problem of the partisan, self-selecting news drip. In 2016, the *Wall Street Journal* launched Blue Feed, Red Feed—an online interactive feature that showed visitors liberal and conservative Facebook newsfeeds side by side.[12] It revealed to them what the other side saw on several issues or keywords: President Trump, health care, guns, abortion, ISIS, the budget, executive order, and immigration. Clicking through, the same Blue Side sources appear again and again, issue to issue on the Blue Side, and same Red Side sources appear again and again, issue to issue on the Red Side. But the two never meet. It is like viewing newsfeeds from different countries—or planets.

The danger of the agenda-setting effect for good political decision-making is that while it might be rational to let the media decide what we should think about, the range of issues we consider are being driven either by a few central bodies (as in the era of broadcast news) or many decentralized but partisan or specialized bodies (like today, in the internet and social media era). And not all of them are acting in the public's best interest, either because they deliberately wish to manipulate us or because the sum of their activity ends up being accidentally distracting or misleading.

Because we lack the time, skill set, or motivation to figure out for ourselves what to pay attention to, the whirl and swirl of day-to-day politics encourages us to make fast, lazy judgments and decisions behind which there is little rational, autonomous effort. We risk becoming pawns in a political game played between larger players over whom we have limited control. And that is bad news for good political decision-making.

Priming

Framing is about *how* information is presented to us, about the way in which it is packaged and communicated. Agenda-setting is about *how much attention* is paid to an issue and, consequently, whether we think it is important. Priming, however, is about the *context* in which information is conveyed. It is most often talked about in terms of how the media can affect how we evaluate politicians or issues. Shanto Iyengar, the political scientist we met earlier, explains that priming is "a process by which news coverage influences the weights that individuals assign to their opinions on particular issues when they make summary political evaluations." More simply, priming influences which criteria are used and how much importance is assigned to them when assessing politicians and the issues of the day.

There are other sorts of priming, but for now I want to focus on the summary political evaluation bit. This might include who to vote for or what to think about an issue—or whether to vote or think about an issue at all. Iyengar identifies priming as an extension of agenda-setting, but they're distinct phenomena. Agenda-setting effects help us decide what is important or not. Once it's been established which issues we are going to pay attention to, priming effects help us decide how to judge them.

So the media has an awfully important effect on how we think about politics and the sorts of political decisions we make. Politicians know this, and so they try to control the news cycle—the sorts of stories that circulate on a given day or week or month. The media, of course, plays a central role in that process. It may accept or reject the issues the politicians want them to focus on, or it may unearth issues or scandals the politicians desperately want to keep hidden. In this way, it sets the news agenda and drives what we think about and how we think about it.

Like agenda-setting, priming works by capturing our limited, selective attention, providing an *accessible means* by which we can judge an issue or a politician. Like agenda-setting, priming effects are neither universal nor inescapable, but they are pervasive. Just as the media determines what many of us will pay attention to, they also determine the criteria and relative weights we place on judgments. They do this by choosing what is talked about, how often it's talked about, and how it's talked about.

The same problems apply here as in the case of agenda-setting: the media makes mistakes; the information sphere is increasingly polarized, polluted, and partisan; and politicians try to game the news cycle—and sometimes succeed. And most important of all, we as rational, autonomous citizens ought to be the ultimate arbiters of how we judge politicians, and that judgment should be based on criteria that are more robust than, "Well, it's what came to mind!"

Priming does not work on "eureka moments." It's not as if, when we are asked about a political issue or cast a ballot, we realize that we have been directed by framing, agenda-setting, and priming. These media effects work on us unconsciously so that when we must make a political decision, we just make it. Then we tell a story — which we believe — about how we got there, often including facts or "facts" and all kinds of window dressing. Consider Iyengar's conclusion that persuasion — that is, changing someone's mind — is rare: media effects are mostly about commanding attention and changing the criteria for judgment, not changing minds.[13]

Let's look at an example of how priming might affect politics: the 2016 US presidential election. Consider this question: if the media had not obsessively covered Democratic Party presidential nominee Hillary Clinton's use of a private email server during her time as secretary of state, would Donald Trump have become president? The question is a bit unfair — so much was going on during the election — but my goal is to get you to consider how important the email server story was relative to how much attention it received and to its impact on the outcome of the election.

By focusing on the email controversy, the media set the agenda and primed voters to judge Clinton based on (among other things) a serious lapse in judgment that was ultimately blown way out of proportion considering the many other election issues, such as health care or trade, that received less coverage. It will take years to fully understand how the email issue affected the election — and we may never know for sure — but so far it seems that the effects of the story coverage were significant. This is especially true given the role played by former FBI director James

Comey, who released a letter about the investigation in the last two weeks of the presidential campaign. The election ultimately came down to a tiny margin, and in the dying days of the contest, the winner was anything but decided.

Later, Clinton blamed her loss on the Comey letter. She believed, as *Washington Post* correspondent Anne Rumsey Gearan tweeted, that it stopped her momentum and energized Trump voters.[14] Is that true? Well, there were other problems with the Clinton campaign. The Comey letter might have tilted the election in Trump's favour at the last minute, but it does not excuse other campaign errors and structural issues in American political life (for instance, sexism) that affected the outcome. Still, Clinton was not alone in thinking the letter might have made all the difference.

Nate Silver, statistician, election expert, and founder of the website *FiveThirtyEight*, wrote in May 2017: "The Comey letter probably cost Clinton the election."[15] He bluntly stated: "Hillary Clinton would probably be president if FBI Director James Comey had not sent a letter to Congress on Oct. 28." Silver's argument is not bluster. He ran the numbers and quantified the effect of the letter, pegging it at a 3 or 4 per cent move toward Trump, enough to swing at least four, and perhaps six, states to him — decisive in a race that was won by less than 1 per cent in three of those states (Michigan, Pennsylvania, and Wisconsin).

But the Comey letter affecting a close race is just half the story. The other half is the lack of media coverage of their role in the affair *after* it had likely decided the outcome of the election and Trump had become president. Here Silver points his finger at the journalists:

> If Comey's letter altered the outcome of the election, the
> media may have some responsibility for the result. The
> story dominated news coverage for the better part of a
> week, drowning out other headlines, whether they were
> negative for Clinton (such as the news about impending
> Obamacare premium hikes) or problematic for Trump
> (such as his alleged ties to Russia). And yet, the story

didn't have a punchline: Two days before the election,
Comey disclosed that the emails hadn't turned up
anything new.

The media may have some responsibility? Silver reminds us that coverage
of the letter "dominated news coverage for the better part of a week." If it
dominated the news, it distracted from other issues. The disproportionate
coverage of the letter thus shifted attention away from other important
stories—the debates, for instance, or the *Access Hollywood* tape in which
Trump bragged about sexually assaulting women. As the agenda changed,
and Clinton's poll numbers quickly dropped, the Comey letter story
continued to hang around for days—critical, final-push days. Clinton
lost three points in a week as voter preferences changed and undecided
voters made up their minds. And then? Crickets.

Those who made up their minds or changed their preference because
of the Comey letter, or the related considerations it brought to the top
of the mind for them, are real-life examples of the agenda-setting and
priming effects at work when the stakes are highest. Absent the letter
and the media's coverage of it, Hillary Clinton might well have become
president of the United States. What if voters had taken their time with
the issue? What if they had weighted the email scandal proportionate
to how serious it was and what it implied about Clinton *relative to* what
other, older but nonetheless serious scandals implied about Trump? What
if the Comey letter had been a month earlier and was not top-of-mind for
voters as they made decisions in the dying days of the campaign? I suspect
the outcome of the election would have been different—as would have
the subsequent, often very difficult years in American politics.

Okay. So the world is whirling and swirling around you. You wish your
days looked like the sky in a Monet painting, but most of them resemble
Kandinsky or Pollock. Messy. And yet you are routinely tasked with
making all kinds of decisions, including political decisions. You need to

decide what to think about this or that issue, whether to engage in debate over this or that proposition, who to vote for in local, provincial/state, or national elections. Moreover, many of these decisions you are meant to make require sophisticated skills and information. What are you to do?

Humans are what are known as "cognitive misers." That is what the psychologists say, anyway. Perhaps reading the word *miser* springs to mind the grizzled visage of Ebenezer Scrooge, the classic Dickens character known best for pinching every pound, shilling, and pence. Scrooge the miser carefully and heartlessly protected his wealth; cognitive misers do the same, but with thinking.

Conscious mental processing is time consuming and tiring and finite. There is only so much thinking you can do before you reach diminishing returns and, eventually, need to take a break and recharge. One way to conserve mental resources is not to think much at all. Another approach is to use mental shortcuts, known as heuristics, to save time and energy when making decisions. Heuristics are also sometimes known as rules of thumb, common sense, or intuition. Daniel Kahneman, whom we met earlier, one of the foremost scholars of heuristics, defines them as "a simple procedure that helps find adequate, though often imperfect, answers to difficult questions."[16] For me, "mental shortcut" is the best descriptor of heuristics, since that is precisely what they are—shortcuts to getting *an answer*, even though it is not always the right or even the best answer. Indeed, as we will see, sometimes we get to *terrible* answers, but not always. And that is part of the reason why heuristics won the evolutionary lottery to be hard-wired into our brains.

When heuristics work, they are a godsend. Even if we had two or three times as much time as we do now, we would not be able to learn and think about *every* important political issue on the docket. But we can strategically choose a few sources we trust—an expert, a professional association, a non-profit—and rely on their judgments to help us form our own impressions. We do this all the time. And sometimes it works.

Back in the 1990s, political scientist Arthur Lupia studied voters in California who were tasked with voting on five insurance-reform initiatives. The Golden State has regular direct democracy, so its citizens often find themselves voting directly on legislative matters, some of which are quite complicated. What is a busy voter with limited resources to do in this case? Become an expert on insurance? Or take a shortcut?

In his study, Lupia found that voters who had little factual knowledge of the insurance initiatives could rely on their knowledge of industry preferences to approximate the sophistication of those who knew more about what they were voting on. Now, that might spook you. Indeed, you might be tempted to worry that this approach turns voters into industry zombies, brainlessly following the diktats of the suits. But that is not the point Lupia is making. "If we believe that well-informed voters make the best possible decisions," he suggests, "then the fact that relatively uninformed voters can emulate them suggests that the availability of certain types of information cues allows voters to use their limited resources efficiently while influencing electoral outcomes in ways that they would have if they had taken the time and effort necessary to acquire encyclopedia information."[17]

That is a good news story. Sort of.

Well-executed heuristic judgments save time and effort. Sometimes they even allow folks with little knowledge to reach judgments that approximate far more informed and sophisticated individuals. So, in some cases, a little good information — and knowing where to look — goes a long way. But when heuristics do not work, they *really* do not work, leading to structural bias, injustice, suboptimal outcomes, and serious challenges to democracy. For example, racial or gendered discrimination can occur in certain hiring practices, with some employers potentially using a person's name as a heuristic.

A 2011 paper by researcher Philip Oreopoulos published in the *American Economic Journal* asked "Why Do Skilled Immigrants Struggle in the Labor Market?" For the study, Oreopoulos sent out 12,910 similar resumes by email to 3,225 online job postings in Toronto, Ontario. Each resume was one of four types: an English-sounding name with a Canadian education and experience; a Chinese, Indian, Pakistani, or Greek name with Canadian education and experience; a Chinese, Indian, Pakistani, or Greek name with foreign education and Canadian experience; and a Chinese, Indian, Pakistani, or Greek name with foreign education and foreign experience.

Oreopoulos found that resumes with English-sounding names were nearly 40 per cent more likely to be called than those with foreign-sounding names. He points out that determining why discrimination occurs is tricky—it could be prejudice-by-heuristic or it could be "rational discrimination" by employers who are relying on an applicant's name to make inferences about candidate skill. But he also conjectures that based on the evidence it is reasonable to argue that it is unintentional, unconscious discrimination driven by stereotypes at work. At the very least, we have reason to be worried about the implications of employers using surnames as heuristic-sorting mechanisms.[18]

That's an example from the business world. But how might heuristics lead us astray when it comes to making *political* decisions? Let's look at party politics for an example. Today's democracies are complex, confusing entities, and their politics match them. For most citizens, the time and intellectual cost of following politics and making political decisions is high enough that they need to rely on heuristics to help get the job done. One convenient and effective heuristic is partisan affiliation. Most democratic states conduct their electoral and legislative politics along partisan lines, with political parties formed to aggregate interests (or to promote some issue or policy agenda), to compete in elections, and—if they are electorally successful—to govern.

For many citizens, political parties offer helpful cues that allow them to sort out what to pay attention to or whom they are going to support. In Canada, voters look at the parties on offer and conclude that the New Democratic Party is on the left (they want to spend money on government programs for everyone), the Conservative Party is on the right (they want to cut taxes), and the Liberal Party is somewhere in the middle (they want to do a little bit of everything). In the United States, the Democrats are left wing and the Republicans are right wing. Sorting parties on the old left-right political spectrum is a blunt approach to understanding a complex phenomenon, but it still helps people make meaningful sense of the political world. Well, again, sort of.

While political parties can serve as a useful heuristic, partisan identity can lead to a different outcome altogether. When someone *identifies* with a party and makes decisions based on that identification—who they vote for, what sort of policies they support or oppose, even who they associate with day to day—they make their party affiliation *part of their identity*. This phenomenon is extremely powerful. And in situations where a country is deeply polarized, such as the United States today, politics can quickly be reduced to base tribal warfare that has very little do with policy even though it has everything to do with politics.

In their recent book *Democracy for Realists*, political scientists Christopher H. Achen and Larry M. Bartels call party attachment "the most important political identity of all," citing "partisan loyalty" as "a common, uniquely powerful feature of mass political behavior in most established democracies."[19]

You might be inclined to defend party identification. Each of us is trying to make sense of the world, alone and together. Few of us are experts in politics—few have the inclination, fewer still have the time for that. So when we map the world, we set markers to help us find our way. Parties serve as some of those markers. What's wrong with that?

Well, partisan identity can lead us towards bad political decisions in a few ways. The first is by shaping our perception of the world. A 2010 study of the US presidential cycle from 2000-04 by political scientists Geoffrey Evans and Mark Pickup found that perceptions of the state of the economy were an *effect* of support for the president rather than a cause. In the research paper, aptly called "Reversing the Causal Arrow," the researchers dug through several years of data from the American National Election Studies—an ongoing survey of US citizens. They looked at presidential approval of Bill Clinton and George W. Bush during those years, whether people approved or disapproved of how they were handling their job as president, and whether that approval or disapproval was strong or not strong. They also examined responses to the question "Would you say that over the past year the nation's economy has gotten better, stayed about the same, or gotten worse?" and the parallel measures of degree: "Much better or somewhat better?" and "Much worse or somewhat worse?" Finally, they categorized respondents by the party with which they identified—Democratic, Republican, or independent—and whether that identification was strong or weak.[20]

It would be fair to assume that politicians are punished or rewarded based on their performance. It would also be fair to assume that individuals can assess the world around them, for instance how well the economy is performing, and assign praise or blame accordingly. So if the economy is doing well, they should be more likely to vote for a politician who is currently in office (as a reward), and if it is doing poorly, they should be more likely to vote against him (as a punishment).

But this is not what Evans and Pickup found.

They discovered that "economic perceptions are derived from political preferences." So what voters thought of politicians affected their perspective on the state of the economy more than the state of the economy affected their approval of politicians. For example, if a person was a strong Democrat who thought Bill Clinton was doing a good job, she was more likely to think that the economy was also doing well, regardless of what the economic numbers of the day suggested. The same was true for a Republican booster of George W. Bush. Our political identities shape our perceptions of the world, rather than the other way around. We see the world through a partisan lens.

Welcome to heuristics gone bad.

We are not always *rational* creatures, plainly. Often, in fact, we are *rationalizing* creatures.[21] When it comes to politics, we frequently operate on autopilot, (blissfully) unaware of the irrational, affective, deep-seated commitments that determine our preferences and votes—and unaware that we are unaware of them. When we are pressed to explain ourselves—what we want, what we believe, and why—we are sometimes able to do so, but often poorly and disingenuously. You will have noticed by now that the person I am describing here is a long way from the sort of ideal good political decision maker I described earlier. We are not by nature the rational, autonomous thinkers that I think we need to be to make good political decisions. But that does not mean we cannot do better.

5. Our milieu

Earlier, I said that we make bad political decisions because our evolutionary capacities for rationality and autonomy are poorly suited to good political decision-making and are further undermined by the world we live in. Remember the Lamborghini trying to make it up the snowy mountain road? Inching forward, sliding sideways and back, passengers hanging on for dear life the whole time. There you have it: us trying to make good political decisions in liberal democracies in the twenty-first century.

Now consider the conditions under which we tend to make the best decisions about complex issues, political or otherwise. We do best when we have lots of time and resources at our disposal, plenty of motivation to reach a good decision, sufficient information to decide with (but not *too much* information), little or no animosity towards other individuals or groups who are involved in or directly affected by the process, few or no strategic actors involved who are trying to manipulate us, and not so many decision options that we become paralyzed by choice. The world we live in rarely provides us with *any* of these conditions for decision-making, let alone many, or all, of them. Can you remember the last time you were frozen in place in the soup aisle of the grocery store, eyeing the twelve kinds of chicken noodle? Or the last time you had to make up your mind about an issue that you were unfamiliar with, and so you set out on a search to learn about it?

Next, think of the sorts of lives we tend to lead. We are always hustling and tired. We have ten thousand things to do during any given day. We are competing with others. We are strapped for cash, and our attention is divided. We have rivalries and hostilities towards others that just will not go away. We either have too little information or too much. And on top of that, we must make our decisions *now, now, now!* so we either make hasty calls, or we procrastinate and never get around to making a choice or go with the default option. Plainly, our lives are not exactly ideally suited for good political decision-making.

But what is driving our frantic world? Who or what is behind all the craziness? Does it have to be this way? Surely not. Our lives don't *have to be* like this.

To some extent, the way we live is a choice we have made — perhaps not as individuals, but collectively we have chosen this. We could have chosen otherwise (not choosing or letting others choose *is* a choice). But what do those choices entail? Where do they come from? How are they shaped? Part of the answer is that they come from and are shaped by the world around us, what I am calling our milieu.

For many of us, our lives are shaped by structures we cannot control, or else can only control in very limited ways. Our milieu conditions not only us mere mortals but also the institutions within it. So if we want to figure out why we make bad political decisions and how we can make better ones, we need to understand what makes up our milieu.

Speed

Let's start with speed. The milieu of twenty-first-century Western democracies is marked by a pace of life never seen in human history. To a person born in, say, the twelfth century, life would have been *slow*, whether they noticed it or not. Nine hundred years ago, it took a long time to do just about everything. It took ages to travel long distances, to communicate with those not in our immediate vicinity, to build things.

As we accumulated technical and scientific knowledge, we applied our discoveries and inventions to life in a way that has speeded things up. Journeys that once took weeks or months now take hours. In the eighteenth century, it took more than six weeks — and often much longer — to cross the Atlantic from Europe to North America, if you managed to survive the journey. Today, a flight from London to New York takes about eight hours. Even in the nineteenth century, prior to the invention of telegraphy, a speedy message by Pony Express, a mail service, would take ten days to get from California to Missouri.[1] In 2013, researchers in the United Kingdom created a fibre-optic network that could transmit near the speed of light — at 99.7 per cent the speed of light, in fact. That's about 299,792,458 metres per second. At that speed, a message would be delivered between Los Angeles and Kansas City before you finished saying the *P* in Pony Express.

What is wrong with that? A few things. First, doing things faster means doing *more* things, which I will say more about in a moment when I talk about volume. The implication of "faster and more" is that we have less time to make any single decision. For some decisions, a lack of time isn't a problem — "Is that a jaguar in the bushes? Who cares? Run!" or "Do we cook tonight or order in...Hello, Domino's?" But when it comes to making political decisions, time is your friend because it takes time to collect information, to learn it, to reflect on it, and to decide on it.

Excessive speed encourages us to use heuristics — when you are expected to get something done quickly, take a shortcut — and to over rely on System 1's quick-thinking strategies. As I said earlier, automatic, intuitive decision-making strategy works well sometimes. But when it does not work, which is often when faced with complex tasks, it *really does not* work. So being able to override System 1 and to think rationally, autonomously, and deliberately is important. When life is sped up beyond a certain point, however, that becomes especially difficult. The very nature of our brains is such that we are constantly making speed vs. accuracy trade-offs with a propensity to tilt towards making faster, easier decisions that rely more on heuristics and less on reason.

Volume

As if speed didn't create enough of a problem for us, the *volume* of information that we must process on any given day is overwhelming. As impressive as we may be as a species, we are not particularly well equipped for processing vast amounts of information — or remembering it. That is why we invented written language, to help us keep track of stuff and to recall it when necessary.[2] Since then, we have used our environment to build all kinds of apparatuses to help us process, index, and store information. But it just keeps coming at us. The information age has put more potential knowledge immediately at the fingertips of billions of us — an estimated three billion people were using the internet in 2015 — than could even have been *conceived of* just centuries ago.[3] Our old friend heuristics can help us manage information, but that strategy comes at the cost of having to rely on others — who have interests and goals of their own — to do the sorting and managing and choosing for us, or to risk making the sorts of mistakes that come with taking shortcuts.

If we want to maximize our control over our own political decisions, then we need to find a way to wade through the ocean of information that is constantly threatening to drown us. Neuroscientist and psychologist Dan Levitin sums up the deluge in his book *The Organized Mind: Thinking Straight in the Age of Information Overload*, giving us a sense of just how much information we must process now — and how much *more* that is than in the past:

> In 2011, Americans took in five times as much information every day as they did in 1986 — the equivalent of 175 newspapers. During our leisure time, not counting work, each of us processes 34 gigabytes or 100,000 words every day.... We have created a world with 300 exabytes (300,000,000,000,000,000,000,000 pieces) of human-made information. If each of those pieces of information were written on a 3 x 5 index card and then spread out

side by side, just one person's share—*your* share of
this information—would cover every square inch of
Massachusetts and Connecticut combined.[4]

That's a lot of information, especially since Levitin adds that the amount
of it we can process per second is about 120 bits (there are eight bits
in a byte and one billion bytes in a gigabyte), which means "you can
barely understand two people talking to you at the same time." That's not
that much; it's no wonder we get into trouble when we're overwhelmed
and try to make a decision. As Levitin put it to me in an interview in
November 2017: "When we reach a point of information overload, when
we're asking our brains to deal with more than they can handle, one of
the first things that goes out the window is patience, as well as systematic,
rational thinking." And with certain tasks, the challenge of processing
all that information is even *more* difficult. In 2009, Fermín Moscoso del
Prado Martín from the Université de Provence found that when it comes
to certain discrete lexical (word-based) decision tasks, brain processing is
only about sixty bits per second.[5]

In a world defined by breakneck speed, the overwhelming volume of
information that we produce offers a particularly daunting challenge to
those who want to take it all in before making a political decision; you
do not have the time to process all the information you might want to
before deciding.

Choices

On top of those piles and piles and piles of information, each of us also
faces a greater range of *choices* than ever before. Choice is where the rubber
hits the road; all that information out there is *for something*, and a lot of it
is meant to help us understand the world and to choose from among the
many options we are presented with. Not all of our choices are political,
mind you. The sorts of choices we have on offer range from the mundane

to the critical: thousands of products each with several brands, a bunch of streaming services offering thousands of television programs and movies, a handful of gyms and ten times as many workout routines, millions of books, dozens of schools, plenty of partners, endless career options.

It is a lot to take in.

In *The Paradox of Choice*, psychologist Barry Schwartz argues that we have *too much choice*. He says "less is more" and "We would be better off if we embraced certain voluntary constraints on our freedom of choice." A certain number of options are good for us, but the value of plurality declines quickly when we must compare too many options, which quickly becomes, quite literally, a case of *too much information*. As he summarizes it, when it comes to information overload, "Having all the world's information at your fingertips is as good as having none of it."[6]

Since the 1950s, Hick's law, also called the Hick-Hyman law after the two psychologists who first codified the idea, has influenced researchers in their study of the rate at which we make decisions from a range of possible choices. Basically, it states that the more choices someone has or the more uncertainty is involved with a choice, the longer it takes that person to decide. Moreover, the length of time it takes to decide increases logarithmically with the number of choices. These days, the law is applied in user design, especially digital considerations such as website or video game menus, to reduce the time users spend thinking about what to choose, and to get them playing, reading, purchasing, or whatever. The abiding thought that underlies it is: keep options limited and choices simple. We often ignore that advice.

Of course, when it comes to politics, there is not *always* a broad range of options. For instance, Americans still have just two major parties to choose from: the Democratic Party or the Republican Party. Canadians have a few more, but only the Liberal Party and the Conservative Party have formed a government federally. Local elections can be trickier, however, especially in Canada where most local elections are not run under a party system. This means that voters must choose from individual candidates—occasionally several of them—without the guide of party alliances. Still, for most elections, citizens have a narrow range of options to choose from—fewer than they do when choosing a brand of coffee beans. I spoke to Schwartz in the winter of 2017, and he pointed out that, unlike his work on consumer behaviour, voting in American politics "isn't like buying jam or jeans." He emphasizes that citizens in the United States "have too few options." But he quickly added that Americans are open to other influences that make good decision-making difficult—like manipulative ads.

But which political party or candidate to vote for is not the only choice citizens face when making a political decision. There are choices about which news stories to pay attention to and which media outlets to visit, which level of government to worry about, which politicians are worthy of your time, and what to think of the environment, taxes, schools, jobs, roads, health care, social assistance, assisted suicide, national defense, the debt, pipelines, trade, and so forth. Added up, these choices, along with the mountains of information that accompany them and the speed at which the news cycle moves, all become a bit too much.

Diversity

The choices we make, especially political choices, affect our fellow citizens, and those fellow folks are a diverse lot: politically, socially, culturally, sexually, ethnically, philosophically, religiously, and so on. One of the major accomplishments of countries like Canada and the United States is that they have made space for a pluralist society in which all kinds of people can come, join, and disagree while living together in relative peace and prosperity.

Unfortunately, there are serious limits to pluralism in practice and plenty of blind spots in which systemic discrimination and inequality govern unchecked. Racism in the United States and Canada towards Indigenous peoples and ethnic minorities remains all too common. So too does economic exploitation. And the balance of power in society often tilts far too much towards the wealthy and those who find themselves within the inner sanctum of industry, government, or even civil society. This failure of equality is known as biased pluralism, where a few groups tend to get what they want way, way more often than others.

Nonetheless, life in contemporary democracies is diverse in all kinds of ways. This leads to deep and persistent disagreement about what ought to be done. This is not a bad thing, however. Non-violent disagreement is important in a democracy. Through disagreement and debate, we work out different solutions to our problems, and we make space for individuals and groups to chart their own course, within certain broad limits—such as we did in Canada during the 1980s amidst a heated debate over the future of the constitution, which led to the creation of, among other things, the Charter of Rights and Freedoms, which has become a model for the world. Disagreement backstops our freedom, too. Three of the core political rights that make democracy possible are the right to free speech, the right to disagree, and the right to make that disagreement public.

Diversity—and the disagreement that follows from it—is a fact of life in a democracy. The way we manage disagreement, however, will make the difference between living together in a peaceful, constructive, and just way and the sort of belligerent unitarianism that leads to and feeds off polarization, abuse, hatred, violence, and systemic oppression. The need to manage disagreement in the face of diversity is a good problem to have, given that the alternative is some other arrangement in which diversity and disagreement are not tolerated. But this need also puts pressure on citizens and government to ensure equity and equality are built into our social, political, and economic lives—something we are not always particularly good at doing. The very nature of diversity and disagreement is such that it makes political decision-making more difficult.

Complexity

So our world is speedy, full of information, and teeming with diversity and choices. It also happens that many of the matters we are asked to consider and decide on are *complex*. It is tough enough to choose a pair of blue jeans from among dozens of options including size and cut and colour—as Schwartz is tasked with doing in the opening pages of *The Paradox of Choice*—but at least we *understand* blue jeans. They're pants. You wear them. They look good—or good enough—or they do not. They fit well—or well enough—or they do not. Moreover, if you make the wrong call about which pair of jeans to buy—who wants to try them on in the store? Not this guy—the world is not going to end. You can always take them back or let them sit in a drawer or hang in a closet for two years before giving them away. But politics matters a lot more than blue jeans.

The political issues that we are asked and expected to weigh in on are themselves complicated. And while individuals are usually perfectly capable of grasping those issues, doing so takes time, resources, and the motivation to try. You can't just riff when it comes to energy policy or immigration. You cannot learn foreign policy on the fly. You can't wing it on the tax code. Issues that affect millions, or even billions, of people and cut across interests and jurisdictions, draw on knowledge from science and law, and involve dozens upon dozens of stakeholder groups are tough to get a grip on. That does not mean we cannot figure things out for ourselves. But it does mean we need to get the process right.

Given that speed, volume, choice, diversity, and complexity make up our world, it is no wonder that we are satisficers—we tend to think about options for a decision until we reach some conclusion that is *good enough*, and then we move on with our lives. That approach might work for blue jeans, but it is usually insufficient for politics and prone to exploitation and manipulation by clever political or other interested operators. We need to move beyond good enough.

Just because our milieu makes life tricky does not mean that we cannot navigate it or come up with good political decisions. In fact, if we can harness our milieu and use it to our advantage, we can set up a process through which ordinary people can play a regular, exemplary part in self-government. But before we deal with how to develop that process, we must dig deeper into the companion of our milieu: institutions.

6. Our institutions

Imagine yourself stranded on an island thick with vegetation. You have landed on a beach, and you need to make your way inland to find food and to build a makeshift shelter. Lucky for you, you have a little hatchet with you (let's not think too much about how you got here or why you have the hatchet, okay?). What do you do?

You grab your hatchet and push on. It's tough going, but after a while you manage to cut yourself a path through the foliage toward the centre of the island. You find some food. You build your shelter. Later, you decide to return to the beach to see if you can flag down a passing ship to rescue you. How do you get there? Cut a new path? No, of course not. You take the old one. And this time, the going is much easier. As the days pass—still no rescue—the path becomes increasingly trampled down as you walk to and from the beach; the corridor you have made for yourself becomes wider as you cut away the brush a little each time. Eventually, you find that you have created a nice little path for yourself. The path is so good that you cannot imagine taking another route; in fact, you are now dependent on it.

This is how institutions are formed, and how they remain in place. Institutions condition how we think and behave. They set up rules, expectations, norms, punishments, and rewards. They are structures that make life familiar and easier to manage. They are hard to get up and running, but once they have been established, they stick around because they serve a purpose and offer a familiar path. And most importantly for our purposes, they affect how you make political decisions.

Every so often, an old institution changes or collapses or a new one emerges that really changes our political lives. Usually this comes about because we reach a critical juncture. A critical juncture is a moment of uncertainty and opportunity in which, for whatever reason, we have a chance to do things in a different way and some reason to seriously consider doing so—like having no other choice.

In *Why Nations Fail*, Daron Acemoglu and James Robinson explain how the fourteenth-century bubonic plague—the Black Death—struck a great blow against feudalism and empowered labourers in England.[1] When it arrived, the disease carried off so many that the value of labour skyrocketed and with it the bargaining power of workers who used the opportunity—a critical juncture—to demand and receive a better deal from their feudal lords. This critical juncture was an important moment in English history—specifically in the history of the rise of human rights and democracy, and it would have implications for much of the world in the centuries that followed. But that is another story.

Thinking about the world today, about the major social, political, and economic shifts we are witnessing, it seems like we may be approaching another major critical juncture that will change how we think about and practise democracy. But our fate has not been foretold. The future of self-government is still up to us to shape as old institutions are challenged and we begin to dream of new ones that will be more equal, inclusive, responsive, and just. We can get there. But first we need to understand a bit more about what institutions are.

When you hear the word *institution*, you might think of a place, of buildings, of something you can point to on a map, of something with a website you can visit, like a university or a think tank. Those are a sort of institution but not the sort I am interested in. For my purposes, I am referring to *conceptual* structures or processes that enable human survival, social and political stability, and occasional flourishing. Or to put it another way, I am not interested in any physical thing itself, but rather how we do things or how we organize ourselves.

Academics disagree (*shocker!*) over precisely what an institution is, so definitions of the concept vary. But the day is short, your time is precious, and we have a lot to do, so here's my favourite definition of the term: institutions are *the rules of the game*. Or, as economists Arthur Denzau and Douglass North put it, institutions are "the rules of the game of a society [consisting] of formal and informal constraints constructed to order interpersonal relationships."[2] Okay, so there is a bit more to it. Another scholar, Jonathan Turner, writing about *social institutions*, suggests they are "a complex of positions, roles, norms, and values lodged in particular types of social structures and organizing relatively stable patterns of human activity with respect to fundamental problems in producing life-sustaining resources, in reproducing individuals, and in sustaining viable societal structures within a given environment."[3]

The important thing is for us to take these definitions as scholarly ways of saying that institutions are patterns of human behaviour that stand the test of time and become widely accepted by people as rules for what we ought to do, when we ought to do it, and why we ought to do it. From that, all kinds of things emerge, including Turner's positions, roles, norms, and values.

Some institutions evolve naturally, some are designed, and some come about thanks to a bit of both. As Turner says in his own, complicated way, institutions *serve a purpose*; they are good for something, which is why they tend to stick around. Institutions help us make sense of the world, they help make sure that tomorrow looks a lot like today by channeling behaviour and expectations in predictable, familiar ways.

Imagine if each day when you awoke you did not know who would behave in what way, or what you were expected to do and not do at home, at work, at the store, in school, and so forth. You would never get anything done. None of us would. Luckily, institutions give structure to life, they pattern and recreate it. Having institutions is thus essential for many of the things we want from and for our lives: progress, predictability, comfort, abundance, and even justice.

Admittedly, not *every* institution is essential, nor are all of them good. Institutions tend to produce winners and losers by patterning life in certain ways that make some more likely to succeed than others. In extreme cases, institutions can be exploitative and even evil. For example, slavery was a legal institution in the United States (and elsewhere) for centuries. Globally, it still exists in many countries in illicit and quasi-legal forms. It was and remains a morally repugnant institution, serving the interests of a privileged few while exploiting and dehumanizing many.

There *are* important and good institutions, though not everyone agrees on what they are. The family is an institution. So is higher education. The courts are an institution. In Canada, the Crown is an institution that tries to tie the country together. Religion is an institution, and faith traditions contain many of their own institutions within them. The internet is a medium full of new institutions that are becoming increasingly important, such as social media or the internet of things. But I want to concentrate on a few specific institutions that commonly and directly affect political decision-making: political parties, electoral politics, the media, capitalism, and—to stretch things a tad—political ideology. These institutions are important, but they are also dangerous: they are subject to hijacking—accidental or deliberate—that can prey on our cognitive limits, manipulating us for profit or political gain.

Institutions shape our lives. They make some things likely, other things unlikely; they encourage certain types of behaviour and discourage others; they empower sets of individuals and groups and disempower other sets. When it comes to political decision-making, our decisions are largely conditioned by the institutions I have mentioned. We are not powerless before them, nor are our actions predetermined by them as if each of us were a mere drone or a member of the Borg. But they are powerful—indeed, some help determine which nations succeed and which fail—and our lives today would be impossible without them.

In this section, I discuss seven institutions that are central to political decision-making: legislatures and the executive (which are different, but I am lumping them together), political parties, campaigns/elections, the media, pluralism/civil society, political ideology, and the free market/private property. I am cheating a bit with pluralism/civil society and political ideology. Pluralism and civil society are systems, but they sometimes operate like an institution, so I am counting them. Political ideology is a system of ideas and beliefs, a way of interpreting and sorting the world, but it can pattern life like an institution, so in it goes. Exceptions aside, my purpose is to explain how our political decision-making is shaped by the incentives, rules, and norms that come from institutions — or institution-like things.

Legislatures and the executive

In most democracies, legislatures make the laws, and the executive (for instance, the president or the prime minister and cabinet) governs by applying those laws and policies — or "executing" them. That is the theory, anyway. The practice is more complicated, since sometimes legislatures and executives are fused (as in the case of Canada, where the prime minister and his or her cabinet are almost always also members of parliament), so there's plenty of overlap. But even when the legislative and executive branches of government are formally separate (as in the case of the United States), the two influence one another and work closely together. It is very common, for instance, for the American president to champion legislation and try to get it passed through the House of Representatives and the Senate. So together they go.

Politicians have goals. Once they are elected, they try to accomplish those goals. As much as we like to assert that "Each and every one of those bums is in it for themselves," the truth is that many politicians — perhaps most — enter public life because they have a policy area or two they care about, they wish to serve their community or their country, or they have a vision about how we ought to live together that they want to see come to life. Now, you might disagree with this or that policy or agenda, and,

indeed, you may fight tooth and nail to oppose the vision of some politician, but that does not change the fact that politicians enter politics to
shape the world in ways that align with how they think things ought to
be.

Intentions aside, we end up with bad political outcomes all the time:
policies that fail to meet their stated goals, legacy programs that are
impossible to end or even amend, massive blunders that cost fortunes
and sometimes lives. Much of the time, these are policies and laws that
people would rather not have.

Now, if the democratic system is working properly, outcomes should
reflect the will of the population — and those affected by decisions ought
to have their say, one way or another, in deciding how they are made. But
politics is competitive, and a team sport to boot. Politics is also about
power and authority — who has it, who doesn't, who wants it, how it is
used, and what it is used to do. Politicians band together in parties and,
within those parties, smaller groups or cliques. As that happens, interests
are transformed, and whatever intentions individual politicians might
have — good or bad — are filtered through that group dynamic. This dynamic includes party discipline, since political parties must work together
to win elections, pass legislation, or — if they are in opposition — to keep
the government accountable.

In Canada, the critical roles that parties play in our democracy, their
use as vehicles for securing power, and their sensitivity to negative press
coverage means that they tend to be top-down and centralized bodies
increasingly run from the office of the leader. It is not uncommon for
party leadership to discipline wayward members of their caucus by
removing them from prominent roles such as Cabinet, important critic
roles, or committee chairs or, conversely, to reward their loyalty with
those jobs — the carrot-and-stick approach to politics. Sometimes, the
ride-or-die mentality gets way out of hand. In 2017, the Conservative
Party booted a senator out of caucus for *having dinner* with Liberal
prime minister Justin Trudeau. Ahead of the meal, which was a thank-
you to senators who had brought legislation forward on behalf of the

government, the party's leader in the Senate gave Senator Stephen Greene the choice of accepting the invitation or the party caucus. "Well, I want to do both," replied Greene. More quietly, Conservatives suggested the reason for Greene's booting was that he had not been a "team player," and that he had been working too closely with non-Conservative senators. Imagine that.

Because most democratic political systems are partisan and competitive, the ideal of serving for the good of the people, first and foremost and above all else, quickly breaks down. Parties and their elected members want to keep a tight grip on their power and authority, rarely delegating it or sharing it with the opposition, or even the public, unless they must. Very quickly, the logic of "How will this serve our interests?" (for instance, staying in power) becomes a force to be reckoned with. We have already seen the power of partisan interests to shape not only behaviour but even our *perception*. Group interests in a partisan, competitive environment, such as a legislature, can distort the political decision-making process. This can encourage politicians (and their staff) to pursue approaches that are inconsistent with good political decision-making, including how they frame policy to the public, how much they involve the public in policy-making and in which ways, how they treat their colleagues and opponents, and which policies they pursue in the first place.

Canada has been engulfed in a struggle over its energy future for years, and in recent times that struggle has been best exemplified by a battle over a pipeline. In 2013, Kinder Morgan, a Houston-based energy company, began the process of expanding its Trans Mountain pipeline, which runs from Edmonton, Alberta, to Burnaby, British Columbia, carrying oil from landlocked Alberta to the Pacific Ocean and off to foreign markets. The goals of the expansion were to twin the existing pipeline and to ship diluted bitumen to China, where it would receive a better price than in the United States, where the resource is discounted.

Politics in Canada is complicated at the best of times, but in this case, things got really messy. While the government of British Columbia initially supported the project, a change in provincial government from the

BC Liberals to the New Democrats changed that. The new government overturned BC's support for the project, citing environmental concerns. At the same time, some Indigenous communities also opposed the expansion, while some supported it. Environmentalists argued that the oil in Alberta would have to stay in the ground if Canada was to meet its climate change goals of reducing carbon emissions—and, more important, if we were to have a chance at fighting rising global temperatures.

As construction approached and started, tensions rose, court cases were launched, and each side dug in. The federal Liberal government declared that the pipeline would be built no matter what, since it was in the national interest and, according to them, "the environment and the economy go hand in hand." The government of Alberta argued the same thing, adding its provincial interest for good measure. For their part, the opposition Conservatives claimed that Prime Minister Trudeau had bungled the project. The federal New Democrats hedged their bets for a bit but eventually came out against the project. Everyone's political beds were thus made and their fortunes, in part, tied to their positions.

Ultimately, the Canadian government had to purchase the pipeline and take on the project itself after investors at Kinder Morgan got nervous in the face of challenges and delays. As the project proceeded and conflicting views of the law and justice collided, no side had any interest in or incentive to back down.

Now, it's perfectly normal for politics in a democracy to play out across several venues at once, and it's just as normal for different governments within a country, at the provincial or state and federal levels, to disagree with one another. The courts and the streets are places where politics happens—they're part of a democratic system. Just like the ballot box or the town hall. But the process by which the Trans Mountain pipeline was approved through the National Energy Board under the former Conservative government and accepted by cabinet was flawed from the beginning. The undertaking suffered from inadequate public consultation and didn't do nearly enough to include Indigenous peoples. In fact, it was such a mess that once they took power, the Liberals pledged to change the process—although that wasn't enough for them to kill the expansion. And rather than go back to engage the public and Indigenous peoples properly on a controversial project that rests at the intersection of debates over jurisdiction, climate policy, and Indigenous rights, politicians bricked themselves up behind their position and called it a day. This wasn't exactly a case of good political decision-making at work.

Few politicians are keen to delegate too much power to the public or to encourage them to engage deeply in the policy-making process. Politicians guard their power and authority, in part for good reason: they are the ones who are ultimately accountable. But that often leaves citizens, for whom democracy exists in the first place, out in the cold.

Political parties, campaigns, and elections

Political parties try to win elections so they can make law and policy. Whatever their electoral chances, political parties are organizations that aggregate the interests of their members and leadership to cooperate toward the election of at least some of their candidates in the hope that they will have enough power in government to promote their agenda.

So the primary goal of political campaigns is to gain or preserve *power* —and through that power, the right to shape the polity as they see fit. The fact that candidates and parties see elections first and foremost as an exercise in power is important. That means that elections aren't *primarily* about informing the public about every policy on offer (and, keep in mind, parties who win often abandon promises after they take office). That doesn't mean that politicians don't care about policy or the people they serve; they do. But as former Canadian prime minister Kim Campbell is noted to have said (she claims she was misquoted), "An election is no time to discuss serious issues." Elections are not primarily about deciding which policies are best for the city or province or state or country, and they aren't about cooperating to work towards political utopia. Campaigns are about *winning power* so that the party and politicians who run for election can implement an agenda they imagine is good for their constituents. But power comes first, since it is difficult to make law or policy without it.

That is not as dire as it sounds, given the alternatives. Democratic elections—the free, fair, and routine ones—channel disagreement and what could otherwise be a violent struggle for political power. They also keep governments accountable and answerable, since governments that fail to deliver on what the people want or who otherwise behave in disagreeable ways are subject to replacement. Because of elections, and the chance of winning power, opposition parties have an incentive to keep close tabs on the government of the day and respond to policy signals from the population when the government does not.

But things, as always, are more complicated than "The people want this or that and they vote for whichever party or candidate delivers the goods." For one, as we saw earlier, many voters *choose their party first* and then align their policy preferences with those offered by their preferred party. Also, parties work hard to manufacture support for their policy agenda before and after elections—and those agendas can change between elections. Since power—winning elections and re-election—is always a motivation, parties have an incentive to build their platforms on policies that will help them get elected. But they don't always deliver the goods. And while democratic countries have rules about elections, the rules do not ensure the most appropriate, necessary, or rational policies are considered, nor do they ensure that politicians will respect the spirit of the rules or the interests of the public.

Earlier, I discussed Cambridge Analytica, the shadowy firm that no longer exists. The company helped Donald Trump get elected president of the United States. It also helped secure a Yes vote in the British referendum on leaving the European Union—under questionable circumstances. In the aftermath of what many saw as "dirty tricks" by Cambridge Analytica during the 2016 US election, some commentators discussed parallels between the dodgy dealings of the firm and those who hired it and what is probably the most infamous scandal in American presidential history: Watergate.

These days, the suffix *gate* is commonly attached to scandals, drawing on the legacy of the break in at a DC hotel and office complex that brought down Richard Nixon and threw the country into a crisis. There are so many examples of "gate" scandals—some genuine, some hoaxes, some serious, some frivolous—that Wikipedia keeps a list that now runs into the dozens and includes Spygate, Pizzagate, Chipgate, Gamergate, Tripgate, Tigergate, Grannygate, Deflategate, Elbowgate, Travelgate, Pardongate, Fangate, Bingogate, Climategate, and so, so, so many others. But the original Watergate scandal remains the granddaddy of them all, serving as a reminder that no democracy is immune from politicians bending or breaking the rules—even very important ones.

While the origins of the affair stretch back further, the first key moment of the Watergate scandal was in June 1972, when five men were arrested breaking into the Democratic National Committee's headquarters in the Watergate complex, a group of buildings along the Potomac River in Washington's Foggy Bottom neighbourhood. An FBI investigation linked the break-in to then President Nixon's re-election campaign. The botched break-in—an attempt to copy documents and install listening devices—led investigators to discover other "dirty tricks" by the Nixon administration, including wiretapping and other forms of surveillance and investigations into the president's "enemies."

President Nixon tried his best to end the investigation into his dirty dealings. He went so far as to attempt to cover up the scandal, even after the probe had moved to Congress. As the noose tightened, the president took the extraordinary step of firing the special prosecutor, Archibald Cox, who had subpoenaed tapes of Oval Office discussions that Nixon had recorded but refused to release, citing executive privilege. At first, the institutions of American democracy pushed back: the Justice Department resisted the president's overreach, with top members choosing to resign rather than fire the special prosecutor. But eventually, Nixon found his stooge. Solicitor general and acting attorney general Robert Bork—later a Supreme Court nominee under President Reagan, rejected by the Senate in what would be an early sign of partisan battles in years to come—did the deed. But the investigation kept going under a new special prosecutor and an increasingly angry public hungry for impeachment.

Finally, on July 24, 1974, the Supreme Court unanimously ordered the president to hand over the tapes, ruling 8-0 that Nixon could not claim special protection as head of the executive branch. The tapes were made public—except for an eighteen-and-a-half-minute section that had been mysteriously erased.

As people began to appreciate the extent to which Nixon and his team had bent or broken the rules, and as investigators dug deeper into the administration's misdeeds, it became clear to almost everyone that the writing was on the wall: the crimes and the cover-up were about to sink the president. On August 5, Nixon released the "smoking gun" tape in which the president approved a cover-up plan, implicating himself in the scandal and obstructing justice. Two days later, on August 7, facing growing public outrage and certain impeachment and removal from office, Nixon, in accordance with federal law, addressed his resignation letter to his secretary of state, Henry Kissinger: "Dear Mr. Secretary: I hereby resign the Office of President of the United States."

In the end, the United States had faced one of its most significant political and legal crises in its history. Rules had been broken. Norms had been battered. Trust had eroded. Sixty-nine individuals were indicted. Forty-eight of them were found guilty. A president had resigned. And all because of a desire for power and blind commitment to partisan loyalty. But American political institutions managed to get the job done: ejecting Nixon, imprisoning some of the offenders, and preserving democracy. There is no guarantee they would be—or will be—able to pull off such a feat today.

Paradoxically, the very institutions that are meant to produce peaceful transitions of power, to keep governments accountable, and to allow cit-izens to communicate their policy preferences to their leaders are highly susceptible to being gamed for partisan or special interest purposes, which may or may not reflect good policies or good political decision-making. And elections are a downright lousy way to communicate policy preferences.

For one, citizens tend not to have stable, discernible positions in the first place. Next, even if citizens did have stable opinions, it would be hard to infer from the election of a candidate just which of those opinions they wanted to communicate to that person with their vote. Work from, for instance, social choice theory — the study of how individual opinions or preferences are transformed into collective decisions — teaches us that aggregating individual preferences (known as preference aggregation) does not give us a single, stable group preference.

On top of everything else we have just talked about, the official election campaign period in most democracies is usually short, fast paced, and information heavy. We as citizens are caught between warring parties that will do whatever it takes within the boundaries of the rules — and sometimes outside those boundaries — to win. We must also decide whom to vote for while being bombarded with information through frequently changing news cycles. And elections are episodic. They happen at regular intervals and people are happy to forget about them in between. Therefore, most of us do not build the skill set needed to navigate them. This puts us at a disadvantage compared to career politicians and their professional staff, who are accustomed to policy thinking and trained to manage the public.

Elections are a good news story when it comes to maintaining the peace while transferring political power. They also provide a mechanism for accountability. But when it comes to the goal of good political decision-making through clear, informed votes that encourage politicians to give the people the sorts of policies they want, the news is less encouraging. Elections are essential to democracy but they are far from ideal vehicles for producing autonomous and rational decisions.

The media

Without a free and independent media, liberal democracy would not be possible. The media scrutinizes government and elected officials and helps keep them accountable by sharing what it learns with the public. Who has the time and skill set required to effectively attend meetings, talk to their elected officials, pore over policy proposals and bills, to make sense of it all? Almost no one. The media acts at once as a source of information and a heuristic to help us make sense of the political world.

In a small community, you might imagine being able to chat with your neighbour or friends about what is going on, and you would likely be able to talk to leaders directly. After all, some of them will be your neighbours. But once a political community grows, that becomes impossible. Having the media around allows us to scale up the size of the polity — city, province or state, country — while still having widespread access to the information we need to know what is going on and to keep elected and appointed politicians and officials as honest as possible. If political leaders expect to be scrutinized by the media, and if they expect the media to relay its findings to the public, then they have some incentive to play by the rules, to provide reasons for the policies and laws they are pursuing, and to generally behave themselves.

But again, in practice things are a bit more complicated. In North America, partisan and sensationalist media — by no means the majority of media, but enough to cause trouble — encourage supporters of one party or another to head to their corners and to refuse to consider ideas contrary to their own while giving those who pay little attention or who are looking for trouble plenty of fodder for anger or outrage. Of course, abuse of the press is not new.

Partisan newspapers have a long history. So too does yellow journalism. In the nineteenth century, yellow journalism was all about bombastic, sensational reporting, or "reporting." Yellow presses existed to drive sales through exaggeration rather than to provide factual, researched accounts of the events of the day. And matters could get extreme. As the US Department of State's Office of the Historian puts it: "The peak of yellow journalism, in terms of both intensity and influence, came in early 1898, when a US battleship, the *Maine*, sunk in Havana harbor."[4] At the time, Cuba was a Spanish colony, but revolutionaries were pressing for independence and the United States wanted Spain off the island because of its own expansionist, colonial ambitions. In that year, leading proponents of yellow journalism, William Randolph Hearst and Joseph Pulitzer, who had been selling papers on the back of intense anti-Spanish sentiment, used the sinking of the vessel to further inflame tensions, move newsprint, and, as it happens, contribute to the outbreak of war between the United States and Spain.

You might be tempted to conclude that there is nothing new under the sun. But new communication technologies, including social media, mean that living within one's own little world is easier than ever. For instance, filter bubbles (an isolated information space that occurs when online algorithms show you only what they think you want to see) and micro-targeting (focusing ads on specific subsets of individuals chosen by sorting through mass amounts of data) make it easy for people to create islands for themselves. And since there is a demand for it, and because technology makes it convenient to supply, it is easier than ever for misleading, sensationalist, or even fake news to circulate.

The rise of fake news is illustrative. During the 2016 US presidential election, social media provided an ideal platform for the spread of false or misleading news designed to cater to partisan bias or sensationalist desires. A 2018 study by political scientist Andrew Guess and his colleagues estimated that "1 in 4 Americans visited a fake news site from October 7-November 14, 2016."[5] But who were those quarter of Americans? According to the research, 60 per cent of visits were by just 10 per cent of the population—"people with the most conservative online information diets."

Dodgy information practices, both on the supply-and-demand side, are exacerbated when local papers die or are consolidated into media empires, concentrating power over social discourse in the hands of corporate elites, who may or may not have the public interest in mind.

The media is a business and has been for as long as anyone can remember. But media concentration in massive corporate conglomerates that own magazines, newspapers, television stations, and social-media platforms, and that have other holdings and interests that may put them in a conflict of interest with the public good, is a newer phenomenon — at least in the modern era. Take, for instance, Rupert Murdoch, the Australian-born American billionaire businessman who at various times has owned cable, television, film, print, and other businesses that include Fox, FX, *National Geographic*, Sky, Hulu, the *New York Post*, the *Sun* (UK), the *Australian*, HarperCollins, and dozens of others. Or American billionaire and the world's wealthiest person (at least in 2018) Jeff Bezos, who owns the *Washington Post* and the ubiquitous Amazon company, which includes retail, music, and video-streaming services, as well as Whole Foods, Goodreads, and IMDb. He also owns stakes in Twitter, *Business Insider*, and dozens of other companies.

Partisan media, concentrated media, micro-targeting, and filter bubbles make good political decision-making more difficult, since the interests here are a selective interpretation and characterization of the world, not the rational, autonomous discourse we are seeking. If different individuals rely on various but opposed sources of information that are deeply biased in opposite directions, it quickly becomes difficult to debate, discuss, or deliberate about public affairs. After all, if we cannot even agree on the *facts*— remember fake news?— we are in trouble. This would be easier to navigate if we had public institutions that provided space for people to engage, learn from one another, and assemble reliable information for decision-making, but we do not seem to be at that place yet.

Pluralism and civil society

We met the important concept known as pluralism briefly in the last chapter, but a refresher and elaboration would not hurt. The pluralist idea goes something like this: in a shared, democratic political space in which people have different interests, preferences, and commitments, you need a way for decisions to be made—for values to be clarified, for scarce resources to be distributed, for policy debates to be settled. So people come together and form groups to champion their ideas about how the world should be, and they try to get government to make decisions that reflect those ideas. Those groups then head into the public sphere and battle it out, and elect or influence government. What we get is a public (peaceful) struggle to shape the world.

As I said, pluralism is not really an institution. It is a system. But I include it here to help make sense of how civil society functions as an institution related to political decision-making. In a pluralist public sphere, there are all kinds of non-government groups vying for power and influence over outcomes, including corporations, non-governmental organizations, and individuals. Civil-society organizations also play a hugely important role. They include, but are not limited to, neighbour-hood groups, charities, churches, and labour unions.

Civil-society organizations help aggregate interests and work to lobby governments on a variety of community concerns and goals. They are one way that individuals can express their desires to their governments and elected officials. Some civil-society groups are more powerful than others, and, often, corporations are stronger still and better connected to elected officials and their staff. Power often pools in civil society, or fails to be distributed equitably or equally. In many cases this pooling is driven by structural biases or injustices, such as religious or racial intolerance. Recall the idea of biased pluralism, where some sorts of groups get more of their way based on considerations that have nothing to do with the strength of their arguments. When the power to make good political decisions is not distributed equally, biased pluralism emerges and leads to all kinds of problems, including crime and corruption.

For instance, trade unions are a central and important part of civil society. They protect and extend workers' rights and act as a counter-balance to the power of governments and business. They are essential to healthy pluralism. But the history of unions is full of stories of the consolidation of power, deep corruption, undemocratic internal practices, and even (though this is an exception) links to organized crime—in some cases with limited pushback from law enforcement. In their article "Labor Racketeering: The Mafia and the Unions," researchers James B. Jacobs and Ellen Peters point out that in the United States "combating labor racketeering did not become a priority until Jimmy Hoffa's assassination in 1975."[6] Such challenges of corruption by no means tell the whole story of unions or erase their importance (and we can tell just as bad or worse stories about corporations), but it serves as a reminder that when power isn't circumscribed and evenly distributed, it can lead to undesirable outcomes just about anywhere it is found.

Political ideology

Like pluralism, political ideology is not quite an institution, but it kind of functions like one. At its most basic, a political ideology is a set of beliefs that mixes in ideas about how a society works and how it *should* work, leading to how that society, in practice, might get from the first consideration to the second. Ideologies emerge and evolve over time, and as they do they become stories we tell about how the world is and how it should be. Ideologies come to behave like institutions by becoming embedded in or informing other institutions. For instance, in countries like Canada and the United States, liberalism—the ideology, not the party—has become dominant. That means that most people and politicians accept the concepts of a free market, private property, and individual rights as a given in their country.

Curiously, most people are not explicitly or consciously ideological, at least when it comes to voting or giving their opinion about some political matter. When people are asked about their ideology, they tend to give incomplete or incompatible answers. In their book *Neither Liberal nor Conservative*, political scientists Donald Kinder and Nathan P. Kalmoe show that while political elites—politicians, political scientists, pundits—may view the world through a consistent ideological lens, most people do not. Indeed, as the researchers note, in the American context, *party identity* is typically more important than ideology.[7] Most people are more likely to identify with a party and then adjust their beliefs to their party than they are to adopt and stick to a coherent ideological view of the world.

Writing in *Vox*, journalist Ezra Klein uses Kinder and Kalmoe's work to understand Donald Trump. Klein characterizes Trump as a politician who "speaks conservatism with an accent, when he speaks it at all." He reminds readers that the Republican, in the past, praised both Bill and Hillary Clinton, identified as pro-choice, opposed the war in Iraq, and supported Social Security and Medicare. Importantly, he points out that part of the reason Trump won was that pundits and other ideologues assumed that coherent ideology was important to voters, but it is not.[8]

Institutions affect political decision-making by shaping the environment in which decisions are made. They do this by providing a broad set of generally accepted practices and rules that create certain incentives, support certain norms, and condition how we think about politics—for instance, often as an *individual-centred* affair, with your own self-interest placed above the interests of the community. These rules and assumptions about our social, political, economic, and even cultural world are conditioned by ideology, buried deep in ourselves and our society.

The free market and private property

Capitalism is a common economic system, and the one used in many democracies, including Canada, the United States, and the United Kingdom. But there is more to it than that. The nineteenth-century German philosopher and sociologist Karl Marx pointed out that capitalism was, in fact, a *social system* that comprises relationships between capitalists and workers.[9] Two of the central institutions in capitalism are the free market and private property. In this arrangement, individuals are free to own, buy, sell, and trade goods, services, and real estate, as they please. Private individuals or enterprises may also own the means of production—the stuff necessary to produce goods and services for sale.

These economic institutions—part, as they are, of a *social* system of exchange—affect political thinking in a similar way to political ideology. In fact, some argue that capitalism itself is an ideology. Just as liberalism tells a story about who we are and how we got here, not to mention how we should behave, capitalism tells a tale that shapes incentives, preferences, and ways of thinking. The capitalist story, for instance, is the story of personal responsibility, hard work, merit, and individualism. Like any sweeping story that tries to capture the reality of a vast and complex system, not to mention the infinitely complex human beings who are part of it, much of the tale is exaggerated, misguided, or mistaken.

Capitalism thus encourages a kind of thinking that, like any ideology or system, can lead to the tyranny of a narrow band of incentives or assumptions that act like mega-heuristics. This can crowd out alternative, perhaps more appropriate, ways of thinking and sorts of decisions. You don't have to be a revolutionary to think that some of these systems and their institutions might have it wrong or need to be reformed. Moreover, sometimes the story told by the free market and private property is just a little too tidy, a tad too neat. By oversimplifying and entrenching a particular conception of the world, these institutions encourage unidimensional and ideological thinking, even when it is not obvious that is what is happening. What you get is *cognitive autopilot*, which serves us well in some instances—for example, knowing the route to work and taking it, day after day, with ease—and serves us poorly in other instances—for example, when are asked to solve difficult, persistent challenges that require new ways of thinking about the problem.

Institutions and the systems in which they operate make mass democratic politics possible; without them, we wouldn't be able to structure the world in the ways necessary for deciding how we're going to live together. Without them, we wouldn't be able to choose together what to do day to day, week to week, month to month, and year to year. Without them, we would have a hard time managing disagreement. It's a good thing we have them. But as important and useful as institutions and systems are, they're imperfect, just like us, and when their imperfections intersect with our imperfections, we get into all kinds of trouble.

7. Five ways of thinking about thinking

We make bad political decisions because the world in which we make them is geared to exploit our cognitive shortcomings and undermine our rationality and autonomy. That might sound like some grand conspiracy organized by a nefarious mastermind hidden in the depths of some grandiose evil lair, but it is not. Instead, it is the product of how our bodies, our psychology, our milieu, and our institutions happen to lead us down the path to bad decisions.

Building a general model of political decision-making that incorporates all of these moving parts is difficult because there are so many variables and humans are tricky animals to study. But, luckily for us, psychologists and political scientists have developed models of cognition that, when read alongside one another, form a powerful entity that we can use to better understand why we make bad—and good—political decisions. In this chapter, I am going to look at five such models. But rather than just pore through the academic literature, I will imagine each model as a person (or two) at a dinner party. So strap on your feed bags.

You are about to meet the dinner guests, each of whom represents a psychological model: motivated reasoning, the elaboration likelihood model, automaticity, social intuitionism, and system justification. Each character has an interesting story to tell about humankind. Each guest is onto something. Each has something important to say. None of them has the whole story—and, in fact, some people who have a bit to add have not even been invited to the table, since there is only so much space—but that's okay. Their stories are not mutually exclusive. Together they give us a good sense of how and why we make bad political decisions, and they point to some ways that we can make better ones.

Norman, the motivated reasoner

The old Enlightenment story about human beings is that when we are presented with a question or a puzzle, we assemble the facts, think things through, weigh the evidence, and arrive at a judgment. This is a process based on what we call a reasoning chain, which proceeds from evidence to deliberation and reasoning and to a decision. But what if that story has things backwards? What if we start with the judgment and work our way back, using deliberation and reasoning as a convenient story for rationalizing the conclusions that we are motivated to reach for some other unrelated reason? Well, say hello to our first guest: Norman the motivated reasoner.

Motivated reasoning occurs when your judgments are systematically driven, often outside of your awareness, by what is known as goal-oriented or directional considerations. This sort of thinking often occurs because someone wants to satisfy some need other than getting the answer "right." What does that mean? Well, imagine our guest sits down and starts talking to you about politics. He is convinced that immigration rates have skyrocketed—*skyrocketed!*—and that unemployment has risen because of it. You press back. Well, no. Immigration rates have remained steady throughout the years, despite some fluctuation upward to maintain our population rates above the replacement rate. And in fact, you add, the new folks who have arrived have paid their taxes, invested some of their earnings, and opened businesses, so they have been a net-positive gain to job creation. The guest, doubling down on motivated reasoning, protests. "No!" he says. "You should see my neighbourhood! So many immigrants, so many shuttered shops. The other day, I was listening to talk radio..." And that's where you politely move on to chatting with someone else.

When we reason (or "reason"), we are driven by all kinds of competing considerations. Motivated reasoning reflects the reality that sometimes our conclusions are, as psychologist David Dunning puts it, "shaped not only by the evidence the world provides to them but also by motivations, goals, needs, and desires internal to the reasoner."[1] Dunning sorts our penchants for motivated reasoning into three sorts: *epistemic*—our need to establish and maintain a coherent worldview (that is, our need to make sense of things); *affirmational*—our need to believe that we are in control of things; and *social-relational*—our need to see the world as fair and organized.

When we reason about politics—or any number of other things, for that matter—and make our decisions, we are doing more than trying to get to the "correct" or "objective" answer, or some considered judgment based on a deep reading of the best research. We are also trying to maintain a worldview and to make sense of ourselves, others, and our surroundings. We are trying to protect ourselves and maintain control. We are trying to feel safe and good about ourselves. We are trying to find meaning. Talking to Norman, then, you realize that he is less interested in a debate about immigration than he is in trying to make sense of why his world is changing and why he cannot keep up.

Our minds work in funny but comprehensible ways. So even when we do something that seems wacky—like deny what is plainly, objectively accurate—we can discern reasons for that sort of behaviour that make sense. In fact, we have developed a pretty good explanation for the modes of thinking that enable motivated reasoning: online processing and memory-based reasoning. When we engage in memory-based reasoning, we are drawing on information that is stored in our memories; we retrieve past experiences and thoughts, evaluate them, and then put them together to offer an assessment of the situation. With online processing, however, we are relying more on our gut, on a rapid process of retrieving past experiences and evaluations stored as emotional content and applying them to a situation on the fly. This process is, as you might expect, highly subject to bias. As political scientists Milton Lodge and Charles Taber put it, this sort of motivated reasoning leads to the "systematic biasing of judgments in favor of one's immediately accessible beliefs and feelings."[2]

So when this sort of motivated reasoning is used, it is often employed to confirm existing beliefs that help us make sense of and keep the world stable.

If you are predisposed, based on past experiences and interests, to see all conservatives as prehistoric monsters, and you are suddenly asked to give an assessment of the new leader of the Conservative Party, then you are likely to say something like, "Well, you know, he's a bit old-fashioned for my liking. He wants to take us back to the 1950s." Whether this assessment is accurate or not, your predisposition to rely on rapid, emotional responses based on patterns that confirm pre-existing beliefs nudges you towards this sort of motivated reasoning. The chain of reasoning goes something like this: conservatives make me feel bad (emotional impression). Conservatives do not share my values (implicit conclusion). I think of conservatives as dinosaurs (pre-existing belief). This leader is a conservative (new information). The new leader of the Conservative Party is a dinosaur (conclusion) and does not share my values (confirming initial conclusion). Or, imagining Norman talking about immigration, you get: "We need to curb immigration or the country will fall apart!" This is based on: I fear a changing world (emotional impression). It must be because of all these new people who want to change it (implicit conclusion). Immigrants are a threat (pre-existing belief). I have seen three new immigrant families on my block in the last year (new information). Immigrants are everywhere (conclusion), and they are a danger to my way of life (pre-existing belief).

In this process, there is no rational reflection going on, no updating of past impressions and conclusions based on new information. Instead, you get someone jumping to a conclusion. That does not mean that their conclusions are wrong—though they might be. It does mean, however, that motivated reasoning in the online mode tends to bias conclusions towards pre-existing beliefs. This makes sense in a world of scarce time and resources, and overwhelming amounts of information, but it does not lead to the best political decisions. It encourages polarization and makes us vulnerable to being captured by partisan or other parochial interests. There is very little rationality and autonomy at work with this sort of reasoning, and so our decisions are easy to hijack for political purposes — which may serve someone's agenda but not necessarily our own — and it does not make for good political decision-making.

But can you blame us, we motivated reasoners? Can you blame poor old Norman? After all, we are only human. We are busy. We are tired. We are trying to make sense of the world while keeping it all together and doing what is best for ourselves, our family, and those we care about. It is hard to blame the motivated reasoner, though we should not tolerate bigotry. Much of this sort of thinking is driven by *emotion* — what is known as "hot cognition." Human thinking is fundamentally bound up in both emotional and rational processes. But what happens when motivated reasoning, driven by hot cognition, gets into your political reasoning process?

Let's return once more to Norman, our motivated-reasoning dinner guest. After a bit, you come back to talk to him. You've had a couple of glasses of wine; you feel it's time. You decide to press him further on his immigration views. You get right to the point.

"What's your problem with immigrants?" you ask.

He replies: "I don't have a problem with immigrants. I just want to make sure we take care of our own."

You press back. "The fact is that immigration is a net *gain* to our country, socially, culturally, economically —"

"Yes, but," he interjects. You wait. "*In my experience...*"

There it is. Motivated reasoning often amounts to rationalization based on your conditioned — though rarely representative — experience in the world. This includes not only how you argue but also which points you raise and consider, and even the sort of research you do in the first place. It is System 1 thinking: fast, intuitive, easy, but subject to bias. And when that sort of thinking is bound up with big-picture life stuff — the need to make sense of the world, the need to feel good about yourself — then it becomes very difficult to set aside what you *feel* to be good, right, or true. And what is trickiest about this? Much of this reasoning happens *outside of our awareness.*

There are two types of goals that motivated reasoners might pursue.[3] Directional goals, which are the sort we have been talking about, mean defending your beliefs no matter what, protecting your identity, holding on to your preconceived understanding of the world. But there are also accuracy goals — instances in which you are motivated to get the right answer. The latter tends to be far more difficult than the former since it requires more cognitive resources: time, attention, and general effort. Still, people are often driven by accuracy aims or *both* directional and accuracy goals. The trick for making better political decisions is to get the balance right — tilting more towards accuracy goals when possible, ensuring that directional reasoning does not get out of hand — so that we can talk to one another and know what is driving us to the conclusions we reach.

One way to think about motivated reasoning is like this: when that dinner guest sits down, he sits down *as himself.* He is not some reasoning robot. He is a human being with wants and needs and desires and preferences and prejudices. He is trying to make sense of the world and maintain a grip on reality. Psychologically, he will be motivated to do all of that, even while thinking about politics and making political decisions. That impulse will always be there; the trick is to find ways to manage it.

Sarah and Paul, the elaboration likelihood models

By now you might think that no one ever changes their mind. But attitudes and minds can and do change. Of course, sometimes they change because interests change or new, competing prejudices emerge, but those are not the only ways that people change their minds about politics — or anything, for that matter. The elaboration likelihood model (ELM) was developed by psychologists Richard Petty and John Cacioppo in the late 1970s to help us understand how, why, and when people change their minds.[4] This time we are going to look at two guests at our dinner party:

Sarah and Paul. Each of them is going to represent a point along the ELM continuum that measures a person's motivation for what is known as elaborated thought. This is the kind of thinking used to rationally process a complex, persuasive message. Since politics is often complex and premised on persuasion, though quite often manipulation too, this approach fits nicely.

Our guest Sarah represents the central route—a path characterized by effortful, taxing thought that will achieve a "high elaboration likelihood." Paul represents the peripheral route—a path characterized using affect, environmental cues, and heuristics that will bring him to a "low elaboration likelihood." In keeping with our System 1 and System 2 distinctions, Sarah's high elaboration fits with System 2 (the slow, effortful, conscious kind of thinking) and Paul's low elaboration fits with System 1 (the fast, easy, non-conscious—by which I mean outside of your awareness—kind of thinking).

Partway through dinner, someone at the far end of the table brings up politics. Talk quickly turns to a recent proposal to raise taxes to fund the expansion of and increased service for local public transportation. Paul hates taxes. I mean, he *really hates* taxes. He is fond of saying, "Taxation is theft." Sarah does not care for taxes, either, but she is not militantly opposed to them. She would prefer they were lower, however, and that government did not waste money. After a while, someone at the table loudly pronounces: "Public transportation is a public good. The city is growing. We need an affordable, efficient way to move people around, to get them to and from work. It's worth investing in. It's worth the money. In fact, it'll pay us a huge return in the long run while making our lives easier in the meantime."

The table turns to Paul and Sarah. Paul opposes the proposal and, as you might have guessed, he is unlikely to change his mind. He has no interest in being persuaded. Researchers find that when it comes to the ELM, both the situation you find yourself in (say, a heated debate online) and your disposition (say, you tend not to be open to listening to others) are important in determining which route you will take when processing a message that is intended to persuade you. So, for example, the more you "enjoy thinking" as researchers put it, the more likely you are to engage in central-route processing compared to those who do not enjoy thinking. And the greater constraints that are placed on you (perhaps you do not have much time), the more likely you are to use peripheral-route processing. As you would expect, then, both personal psychological considerations and environmental considerations play a role in determining just how open you are to rational reflection when faced with a persuasive message.

This helps explain why not everyone approaches discussions and debates the same way. Paul dismisses the idea. "That's absurd," he says. "If transit wants money, they should find a way to save money! Find efficiencies! Cut the fat! Stop the gravy train! I don't want to pay for some bloated quasi-government organization to waste my money." Sarah, on the other hand, is a high-elaboration candidate in this situation. She cares about public transportation and is not so committed to the idea of low-taxes-no-matter-what that she will immediately dismiss the increase.

Everyone at the table becomes engaged once more in the conversation, exchanging ideas with Sarah. She takes the time to listen to the arguments for and against the tax increase, engaging in central-route processing (that is, System 2 thinking). Most importantly, she commits to *reason-giving* as a kind of conversational currency without presupposing where she will end up on the matter. In other words, she is open to listening to arguments and to making up her mind afterwards. This puts her on the path to good political decision-making, given that she is committed to a rational (and hopefully autonomous) process.

That is good news. It turns out that central-route processing is less susceptible to being hijacked by bias and manipulation — or cognitive error. That makes sense. The more you pay attention, the more you are *open to being persuaded*. That is, the more you're motivated to care about reasons rather than your pre-existing prejudices, the better your thinking — and decision-making — will be. Not surprisingly, researchers have found that persuasive messages processed through high elaboration tend to be more durable and impactful once they are adopted.[5] One of the tricks to good political decision-making, then, is getting people to be more like Sarah and less like Paul.

Stephen, the autopilot

Another trick to making good political decisions is overseeing your own decision-making procedure. When it comes to some things, automatic behaviour is great. Want to hit a baseball? You had better hope that process is automatic, because you do not have time to think it through once the pitcher releases the ball. Trying to play a song on the guitar? If you want to shred, you would need to move from note to note without having to stop and think about what comes next.

That is automaticity. In its simplest form, this refers to the phenomenon of a person being able to do things without thinking about them. Automaticity might remind you of System 1, which makes sense — it is part of your cognitive automatic system. But while System 1 is a *metaphor* for a way of thinking, automaticity includes specific mechanisms that help us understand just what is happening when we jump to a conclusion or fall back on the same old decisions that we always make. As explained by psychologists John Bargh and Tanya Chartrand, automaticity refers to our automatic, non-conscious self-regulation and motivation, and it has implications for political decision-making, including what you care about, the sort of moral judgments you make, and even the issues you pursue.

Of course, we need automaticity for all kinds of things. But when it comes to political decision-making, autopilot — a status which you may not be aware of or able to stop — is rarely your friend.

But what does hitting a baseball have to do with voting for a candidate?

Automaticity is broken into streams, one of which is the *action-perception* stream that Bargh and Chartrand call "the automatic effect of perception on action." It refers to the link between your perception of an action and the actuality of that action. Even though you can control a lot of your own conscious thinking, you cannot consciously control perceptual activity. The world around you influences your thinking and your behaviour whether you are aware of it or not, especially as that sort of perception "introduces the idea of action." For example, think of some spontaneous action or thought triggered by the environment, such as someone's bigoted remarks about race or sexuality. You may react against it instinctively and want to say something, to call out the remarks as inappropriate. This shows how your *environment matters* when it comes to the sorts of political decisions you make. It starts a chain with an environmental trigger that you perceive. The trigger generates cognitive activity that leads to a behavioural outcome.[6]

The second stream of automaticity is the *non-conscious activation* of motivations and goals, which Bargh and Chartrand call "the automatic goal pursuit." This one is a doozy. Part of our idea of what it means to be human is the idea that our goals and the things that motivate us to pursue them are the products of conscious reasoning and deliberate choice. But is that how things really work? What if our environment, the people we spend our time with, and our habits play a significant role in driving our political decisions?

It is finally time to meet our next guest, Stephen. We will not be chatting with him long. He embodies the essence of automaticity in politics. He adopts the position of his party of choice, takes in its messaging, and consistently spits out talking points without thinking about it, like Steve Nash sinking free throws, one after another after another.

Through frequent and consistent pairing, we develop behavioural patterns. Over time, these patterns become deeply encoded in our behaviour, and we forget they exist. Why is it that every time someone suggests that politicians should listen more carefully to their constituents, Stephen replies, "That's not how the system works!" While talking at the table, you discover that he picks fights about politics on social media and engages in name calling with those who disagree with him. Why is this man like this, you wonder, as you look for someone else to talk to. Well, it's because whenever these political decisions—which is what they are—become automatic, they become less rational and, potentially, less autonomous. If the patterns are driven by habit, they tend to produce bad outcomes—they lock in behaviour and produce a cycle of bad decisions: stimuli, response, feedback into the world, repeat.

The final stream in automaticity is the "automatic evaluation of one's experience." This refers to the ways in which our emotions, moods, considerations, and judgments are generated in part or whole by factors outside our awareness. Think of the last time you were in a bad mood. Did you *choose* to be? No, something triggered that mood. Maybe you can point to the reason, but often, you cannot.

The same can be said of the political decisions we make: we need to decide, so we decide. Before we know it, the thing is done. A pollster calls you: "What do you think of the government's new plan to require snow tires between October and March?" And then, instantly, "I'm against it! We don't really need them!" followed maybe by an explanation why. But is it something you've thought about? Have you dug through the data? Do snow tires save lives? How much more is it going to cost you compared to how much safer you and others will be while on the road?

During dinner, you turn to Stephen and raise the immigration question, having overheard Norman talk about it earlier. He stares at you for a moment, and begins, "Well, as the party leader said the other day…" without missing a beat. No reflection. Just automatic non-thought based on a history of repeating talking points.

Immediate automatic evaluations can come about based on a kind of internal tagging system which links ideas, events, or individuals to impressions that we can immediately retrieve when they become relevant to a situation—and sometimes even when they do not. The process of retrieval and evaluation happen instantly and automatically, bypassing rational, autonomous reflection—that is, unless we can catch ourselves and override the automatic impulse to jump to a conclusion. And even when we do catch ourselves hustling towards an answer based on our gut, our more rational and considered evaluations will still be affected—coloured, shaped, clouded—by our automatic judgments.

Earlier we talked about the researchers Charles C. Ballew and Alexander Todorov of Princeton University, who wanted to know if our snap judgments of the facial appearances of candidates could predict the winner of an election. Do our quick, automatic judgments affect one of the most important kinds of political decision-making: who we vote for? According to the story we like to tell ourselves about voting, we take the time to choose the candidate who is best for the job based on *merit* as determined by an evaluation of ideas or the public record—who has the best policies, who is most trustworthy, who has the most experience. But what if voting is, at least in part, a game of "Hot or not?" or, in this case, "Competent or not." Ballew and Todorov found that with as little as *one hundred milliseconds* of exposure to images of candidates (who were previously unknown to subjects) in an American gubernatorial election, people who were asked to judge "which candidate was more competent" predicted the winner of the race more often than not—60 per cent of the time. "The current findings are consistent with the ideas that trait judgments from faces can be characterized as rapid, unreflective, intuitive ('System 1') judgments," the researchers concluded, "and that, because of these properties, *their influence on voting decisions may not be easily recognized by voters*."[7] I added the emphasis in that last sentence to drive home the point that not only are our judgments often made automatically, but they are also made *outside of our awareness*. This upsets the old idea that we are always inherently autonomous and rational creatures.

If some of our immediate perceptions and judgments are shaped automatically and non-consciously, they are shaped *by something*. Some of the forces that do this work are ancient, buried deep in our evolutionary architecture. But other considerations are more recent and contingent on socio-cultural norms or prejudices, such as our racial and gender biases.

Think of the study by Ballew and Todorov I just raised and what it implies: people have an idea of what the "competent" and "winning" candidate looks like. That comes from somewhere; it is a construction. In our dominant social, cultural, and political practices and institutions, systems of power privilege some people over others, affecting our political judgments in the process, rendering them less autonomous, rational, and, importantly, less just.

Stella, the social intuitionist

We like to think of ourselves as decent, moral creatures. Nearly everyone wants to think of themselves as *good*; few people wake up in the morning, look in the mirror, twist their comically long mustaches, and cackle, "What sort of evil shall I do today?" That does not mean that no one ever behaves badly, but most people do not think of their behaviour that way. But we don't just think of ourselves as moral people; we think of ourselves as *in charge* of our moral judgments. For us, it's not enough to be good; we must also *choose* to be good. But do we choose our moral judgments? Sort of. But perhaps not in the way you would expect.

Psychologist Jonathan Haidt has been researching social intuitionism for years. Contrary to what might seem intuitively true, he claims that moral reasoning does not cause moral judgment. This turns on its head the old rationalist model of judgment—the model we usually think about when we think about a "good" political decision: a considered judgment based on evidence, reflection, rational evaluation, and autonomy. Instead, if Haidt is right, the rationalist model has it backwards. People *start* with a gut judgment (recall System 1 thinking) and then work backwards to reason for or rationalize the conclusion they have reached. As Haidt puts it, our judgments are more like "a lawyer trying to build a case rather than a judge searching for the truth."

And while this process occurs in our heads, it is inherently social. Our judgments are affected by the evaluations—and pressures—of others; in turn, ours do the same to them. We are social animals, after all; our survival has long depended on it. In the past, to be thrown out of the group often meant death. We are hard-wired to hew to the opinions of the others who might keep us safe.

After a while, that dinner conversation turns to the subject of assisted dying. (What a political bunch this is!) Throughout the evening, Stella, our intuitionist in the corner, has been quiet. But now she jumps into the conversation.

"It's wrong," she states.

Sarah, the high elaborationist, presses her. "Why?"

"The state shouldn't kill people," Stella says.

Sarah clarifies that it is not the state who assists, it is the doctor, and only under strict conditions, with a patient who is sound of mind, and who chooses to end his or her life. That does little to persuade Stella, who digs in. She tries a few other argument avenues, including the oldest one in the book, "What if doctors start killing *everyone*, you know, to save money or weed out the older population?" Stella is struggling to reason backwards from a moral position she holds, based on a conception of life and our duty to protect it, no matter what.

Moral and ethical norms are important to social order, and it is no wonder that they become established and encoded into how we think and behave over time. In many cases, this process is a very good thing for us, since it helps establish patterns of behaviour that facilitate cooperation and order. However, in some cases, these settled practices and ways of seeing the world can lock in bigotry and hatred, old and less effective ways of thinking and self-organizing, and powerful interests (for instance, political parties and pressure groups). And since the moral judgments that underwrite these things occur automatically and non-consciously, they are tough to interrogate and even tougher to change. In fact, in many cases moral intuitionism takes options off the table, making utterances that question our morality unspeakable and stifling debate and undermining efforts to make more rational and autonomous political decisions. Stella sees assisted suicide as murder. She has made a deep moral judgment based on an emotional commitment to her worldview. She has no intention of changing her opinion. And when moral visions of the world collide, and camps start doubling down on their group's moral intuition, politics risks becoming a mere clash of worldviews with little or no space for discussion or debate. If we cannot engage in good political decision-making on moral questions, then we are in big trouble.

Many of the political issues that people care about the most are either directly or indirectly *moral* issues related to concerns that include the family, the environment, and, of course, freedom. The vigorous disagreements over abortion, same-sex marriage, assisted dying, climate change, the death penalty, poverty, sex work, immigration, and free expression itself are reminders of that. Our moral judgments related to these and other matters are inherently political, since they are related to how we think we should live together. And if they are caused by rapid, non-conscious intuition related to social perceptions, and backed by rationalization, we are likely to get different outcomes than if we had reasoned our way to an answer. In doing so we may shut out other perspectives, making productive exchanges with others much more difficult. This reduces politics to strategy and winner-take-all contests rather than discussion and engagement aimed at understanding and, if necessary, compromise. In Haidt's model, there is rarely hope of transforming deeply held emotional opinions and an ever-present risk of politics becoming a culture war, though I am sure he would admit, as most would, that morality *does* change over time across the population. But in the heat of the moment in a culture war, there is no space—or time—for autonomous, rational political decision-making. There is only time for battle.

Shauna, the system justifier

Whenever you are asked to make a political decision, you cannot help but draw on your own history, context, and other considerations that make up the backdrop of your life and times. Your political decisions are fundamentally rooted in who you are, where you are, and where you have come from. Humans need some measure of structure, familiarity, and predictability to live comfortable lives, and so we develop norms, patterns, habits, and institutions to facilitate those needs. Like I said before, imagine if every morning you woke up and *everything* started from scratch: your religion (or lack thereof), your ideology, the rules of the road, the procedures for filling out paperwork at the office, social cues such as how and when to line up at the bus or the coffee shop, and so on. You would be stressed. You would get nothing done. And, quite frankly, you would be miserable.

The social, political, and economic structures of our lives come together to create systems under which we live and which dictate much of how we behave, including how we treat one another, what we value, and the sorts of behaviour we tolerate and reward: they even help determine the sort of people who tend to become successful and those who do not. While these systems, including class and both economic and political systems, make lives easier to live for many, they also create cleavages, privileging some, shutting out others, and producing structural unfairness and injustices that tend to be reproduced generation after generation. So when it comes to political decisions, there is a constant tension between reform — those who want in, those who want fairness, those who want justice — and the status quo.

That tension is complicated. You might be tempted to think that it's all about interests — the haves and the have-nots battling it out over resources, recognition, and power. And while there's plenty of that, we both maintain and change our systems in complicated ways that include a mix of routine and new political decisions. In psychology, system justification is defined as the "process by which existing social arrangements are legitimized, even at the expense of personal and group interest."[8] Evidence from decades of research into how we make decisions, where our beliefs come from, and how we reach judgments through the lens of system-justification theory reveals that we are motivated — often unconsciously — to hold favourable attitudes towards the status quo, that is, towards existing systems. Sometimes we even hold these attitudes and make decisions to support them that go against our personal interests or the interests of our group (for instance race, gender, or class).

Dinner winds down and it is time for dessert. Shauna finds her way across the table and joins a conversation about poverty. Someone is arguing for increased redistribution so that economic outcomes are more equal. After a while, Shauna offers a rejoinder: "Some people work harder than others, and those people should be rewarded for their efforts." That is a common opinion and it is fair enough. In this case, Shauna herself is a low-income earner, so one of the guests presses her on this. "Don't you work hard, Shauna?" She quickly responds, "Of course I do! And very soon that effort is going to pay off, and I'm going to be rewarded!" Shauna sees the current order as just and fair; she is a temporarily inconvenienced but soon-to-be-member of the middle or upper class.

Luckily for us, not *everybody* is ready to rush headlong into supporting the current order at any cost. But it is common for people to do at least *some* of that. John Jost is a social psychologist at New York University. He and his colleagues put it this way: while there is "a general psychological tendency to justify and rationalize the status quo, we do not assume that everyone is equally motivated to engage in system justification." So system justification, which can encourage people to support unjust and harmful practices, is so deeply embedded in society that not only do *advantaged groups* tend to show more support for their own kind, *less advantaged* groups—consciously or unconsciously—do too, often at a cost to their own well-being and the well-being of their cohort.[9]

When we make political decisions, we are not just deciding in the moment, for the moment; rather, we're making a decision in a particular context that connects the past to the future by extending the life, and the legitimacy, of the systems that shape and structure our world. Unsurprisingly, our motivations to support the status quo run deep, operating implicitly and often non-consciously.[10] System justification reflects a desire to feel good about ourselves and the world, to make sense of things, and to protect against the ever-looming spectre of "what if...?"

Politically, the tendency to make decisions that justify the status quo is particularly common among conservatives. In a 2003 study, Jost and his colleagues found that the essence of conservatism was resistance to change and a commitment to justifying inequality, and that motivations to hold corresponding ideological attitudes were linked to the need to manage uncertainty and threat.[11]

So what? You might say that if we are making decisions that help make sense of the world and that requires preserving the status quo, then so be it. That's just the cost of doing business. It serves an important function: system-justification bias is the glue that holds society together. There are problems with that thinking. First, system justification helps bake in social inequities and injustices. Thus, the "glue" of system justification is more like a wall that keeps some people out. Second, one of the costs of relying on decisions enabled by system justification is that you compromise two of the important factors of political life: rationality and autonomy. After all, when you're justifying the status quo, you're often doing it unconsciously; you're *rationalizing instead of reasoning* and you don't even know it. This forecloses on possibilities of living differently and it robs you of the right to truly decide for yourself how you wish to live.

Now you have met our five models. Remember that none of these models captures every aspect of decision-making, and how people experience the world and arrive at decisions varies from person to person. But these accounts of our psychology capture our tendencies to fulfil psychological needs, tribalism, bias, emotional thinking, non-conscious information processing, and rationalization. This does not mean that we're utterly and hopelessly *irrational* creatures lacking any autonomy or self-control. It does mean, however, that the gremlins tend to sneak into the machine, and we often fail to live up to the ideal of the rational, autonomous decision maker that has been with us for hundreds of years.

More to the point for our purposes, these models also remind us of one of my central arguments in this book: we are not incapable of making good political decisions. But the odds are routinely stacked against us because of our psychological makeup and the way our environment has evolved. That means that we must work for it: we must adopt personal practices and institutional solutions that encourage and facilitate better political decision-making. There is no set-it-and-forget it mode for doing better, which is fine. Doing better means working at it. Constantly.

So let's get to work.

THREE

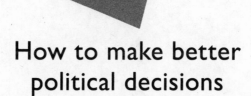

How to make better
political decisions

8. I want you!
(to make better political decisions)

This book is about why we make bad political decisions, what it takes to make better ones, and why it is important for us to do just that. Democracy is under siege from authoritarianism, xenophobic populism, and other regressive forces, and its future depends upon a population that believes in self-government and participates in politics. It also depends on governments wise and just enough to support their citizens as good political decision makers. Our society needs individuals who can rationally and autonomously form preferences, share those preferences, and act on them when they attend a town hall, take part in deliberation, meet with a politician, or cast a ballot. It also needs representatives who trust the people they are meant to serve and respect the value of distributing power to people.

Good political decision-making implies and requires trade-offs, since doing better takes time, attention, and other resources. It also requires that at times we focus on citizen skill-building, including making the resources required available to get that job done. If that seems unreasonable, keep in mind that democracy is premised on the idea of self-government, and without it, we will soon find our way of life going the way of the Carolina parakeet.

You might reply that our style of democracy is mostly representative. That means that citizens elect representatives to govern for them. In Canada, we go to the polls to elect municipal councillors, members of provincial legislatures, and federal members of parliament to represent us. So typically, that means that our elected officials exercise their own best judgments in deciding what sorts of laws and policies to enact. But there's more to democracy than merely sending politicians, as trustees of the public interest, out to serve on our behalf, rewarding or punishing them at the next election. Or, at least, there should be more to it than that.

For democracy to remain resilient in the face of challenges, the outcomes it produces must reflect what people want—or else folks will start to wonder what the point of having a democracy is in the first place.[1] And for democracy to be just, those outcomes must reflect a diverse range of preferences from a diverse range of citizens and residents. This includes regular people who find themselves a part of one minority group or another, not just the social, cultural, political, or ideological majority or elite.

So how do we get there? How do we get to a place where we have more inclusive, participatory, just, and diverse democratic politics built to last? One route is to rely on the majority or elected officials (and other institutions, such as the courts) to do that work for you. This is how most of us have been operating. But that path is fraught with dangers, including a long history of the majority and their elected officials *not* doing that work. In many cases, historically, they have worked *against* that agenda.

Another route takes us down the road of participation. This route passes by a giant billboard that reads: "Who should decide what a policy or law looks like? Broadly speaking, anyone affected by it." This recalls the slogan "Nothing about us without us!" which has long embodied the spirit of the idea that citizens and residents should be an active part of the political decision-making process, especially those who come from traditionally under-represented, oppressed, or marginalized communities, both at and well beyond the ballot box. That slogan has a long pedigree, encompassing ideas of popular sovereignty and self-determination. In recent years, philosophers and political scientists who advance the all-affected-interests principle (which I will call the AAIP from here out) have taken up this call to inclusion. The central premise of the AAIP is that those who are significantly affected by a political decision ought to have a chance to influence its outcome. If, for example, the government proposes diverting a highway through my neighbourhood, I should have a chance to take part in determining whether that is done. The AAIP helps us understand who "the people" are or should be when we refer to "the people" — those who are directly affected by a given political decision that is to be made.[2]

That's all well and good in theory, but what about in practice? How realistic is it to expect people to regularly take part in political life when they have plenty to do already? Well, the idea here is not that *everyone* should *always* be involved in *every* political decision. Rather, it is that members of the public significantly affected by some important decision should have the *opportunity* to help decide the outcome. But to make that opportunity real — rather than just some public-relations stunt or feel-good democracy washing — those folks who are going to be affected by a decision need enough time, money, and skill to make their participation not just possible but effective.

Here we return to the idea of pluralism. Remember that a pluralist democracy is one in which many groups vie for resources and the outcomes they prefer, where interests and ideas about how the world should be are constantly contested. Pluralism captures a fine enough idea: that in a democracy there is going to be disagreement, limited resources, and inconsistent ideas about what ought to be done. Groups and individuals should have to struggle amongst one another and the government in public to decide how decisions should be made and what they should entail.

But recall that in practice, pluralism is flawed. Decades ago, political scientist E.E. Schattschneider summed up the problem when he noted, "The flaw in the pluralist heaven is that the heavenly chorus sings with a strong upper-class accent."[3] What he meant is that the state is not neutral in a pluralist society, nor are the people working to influence outcomes equitably, or even equally, treated, even when it comes to mere equal opportunity.

Imagine that pluralism is a foot race. Some runners start a few metres ahead of their opponents. Others start dozens of metres ahead. Sometimes, a few participants start right beside the finish line. And the distribution of these inequalities is neither randomly determined nor easily remediated. They tend to be carried over from issue to issue, government to government, and generation to generation, placing some groups in structurally disadvantaged positions through little or no fault of their own. This built-in set of advantages biases pluralism and the sorts of decisions that politicians make.

For the AAIP to work in a pluralist democracy—I mean for it to *really work* in practice—resources and opportunities must be more equally distributed among people. One of these resources is the capacity to make good political decisions so that when the time comes, participants in political discussion, debate, protest, elections, and all the bits and pieces that are part of a democracy, can make their decisions count. Achieving this sort of civic capacity is not easy, and it takes structural change as well as personal effort to get the job done. (I will address the structural bits in the next chapter.) But for now, I want to focus on how you—specifically you—might personally make better political decisions, through five practices or techniques that can be used when deciding who to vote for, evaluating a political issue, or participating in a political discussion or debate.

Targeted motivation, or "Eye of the Tiger" on repeat

It should go without saying that one of the most important tools for making better political decisions is the *motivation* to do just that. It *should* go without saying, but it cannot. Making better political decisions requires time, practice, and effort, and these don't tend to come easily, naturally, or accidentally. Making better political decisions requires a commitment to pursuing strategies that shut out much of the day-to-day noise that nudges you towards reflexive tribalism and bias, and it commits you to work to tip the scales of your decisions toward rational, autonomous reflection. That doesn't mean that there's no space for emotion, for your gut. But it does mean that we have to be very honest with ourselves about what we want from politics, why, and what *really* motivates us to want those things.

It is easy for us to live our political life on autopilot: we can pay casual and occasional attention to the news, avoid political discussion and debate, and maybe cast a ballot every few years when someone guilts us into it. It's just as easy to rely on our immediate sense of what we want to make the few political decisions we choose to make: "This candidate feels right," or "This is the way my mom and dad vote." But to make good political decisions, we need to switch off autopilot, do a bit of work in the System 2 mode, and interrogate ourselves a little more than we are used to.

Earlier we looked at the elaboration likelihood model and its account of two ways that a person encounters an argument: a peripheral route full of cognitive shortcuts and gut thinking, along which people tend not to think very carefully about a message; and a central route, along which people scrutinize each message and review their options. It turns out that one of the reasons people choose the central route—the kind best suited to making good political decisions—is *motivation*. You must *like* or *want* to think.[4] For instance, if some issue is relevant to your life, if some outcome will affect you, then you are more likely to take the central route. Think of the difference in time and energy and attention you put into researching and test-driving cars when you plan on buying one compared to when your friend asks you which vehicle she should select, or the sweat and tears you put into scouring a city to buy a home or find a place to rent versus the "Oh, yeah, looks great" responses to texts from eager friends who are doing the same. Motivation matters.

Unfortunately, many politicians and their strategists have no interest in you taking the System 2, central route of rational, autonomous reflection—the route that encourages you to make good political decisions.

They are not interested in motivating you to reflect too much on your reasons for or against them or their positions on the issues. Their job, largely, is to get you onside or at least to suppress your critical response to their goals or suggestions. This is often made easy by the way we organize political and economic life: fast, complicated, partisan, economically unequal, and cutthroat.

This book has been full of examples of such political cynicism and manipulation at work: stories of broken rules, misleading ads, exploitative tactics. But one of the most powerful tools in politics in many countries is money. Indeed, money makes a lot of the other stuff, like ads, possible. Rules about money in politics vary from country to country, province to province, state to state, and even city to city, but federal campaign finance laws in the United States are the poster child for what *not* to do if you want a vibrant, inclusive, deliberative democracy.

In American politics, money comes first. During the 2016 US election, the Democratic side raised $1.4 billion, including money raised by the Hillary Clinton campaign, Democratic Party fundraising, and Super PACs — third-party political action groups.[5] The Republican side and Trump raked in $957.6 million. In total, recorded election spending for the two sides, in a country of about 326 million people, was nearly $2.4 *billion*.

And where did that money go? Not towards fostering an open, honest, constructive democratic conversation, that's for sure.

As election day neared, in late October of 2016, the Clinton campaign had spent as much as $172 million on television ads alone. By November, that number was up to $211 million. And that is just a drop in the ad bucket. As researchers report in *The Conversation*, digital ad spending during the campaign — on social media and other electronic avenues — was up 576 per cent from 2012, reaching a bonkers $1.6 billion. And what was the content of those ads? According to researchers, character attacks. Everywhere you looked, a distracting, misleading ad. Trump as a bully. Clinton as anti-working class. Trump as inexperienced. Clinton as a worn-out insider. A ton of distracting, discouraging, counterproductive focus on the bad and the ugly.[6] And not much focus on healthy democratic discussion and good political decision-making.

In the face of all of that, we must find our motivation to make better political decisions. That may sound like a tall order if you've never thought about it before. But there are some common, fundamental motivations that can be harnessed. The first is that by committing to rigorous thinking about politics, you might come to different, perhaps better, conclusions than you otherwise would have by relying on whatever you already happen to believe. By better, I mean conclusions that either more closely serve your self-interest and/or are more rigorously reached and therefore more likely to be the product of conscious choice rather than accident or habit.

Imagine, for instance, that you've always voted for the low-tax party because you've always believed that it's a matter of freedom: the less the government takes, the more you have in your pocket to spend as you see fit, and you believe that people should be self-reliant, not dependent on government handouts. But it also happens to be in your interests to do so since you have always expected that you would be in a high-income bracket. Over time, you develop an identification with that party, and you form a habit: voting for them.

But what if, like most people, you never find your way into that higher income bracket? What if you would be better served by higher taxes that enable, say, universal social programs such as pharmacare or child care? And what if, upon reflection, you determine that there is a different conception of taxation that you have never considered: that taxes are not only, as is often said, the price we pay for civilization but also a cooperative way to smooth out the inequities and inequalities of the market system, slightly curtailing the freedom of the well-off to enhance (in relative terms) the freedom of those who are less well off? After all, it is meaningless to speak of freedom if you work two or three jobs and can barely afford to feed yourself and your family while keeping a roof over your head. Of course, you could reverse this story, too, and tell it the same way. The point is that rigorous reflection can lead to better conclusions both in narrow self-interested terms and in broader, philosophical terms. Your careful consideration could change your mind, or it could convince you that you do believe what you've always believed—but now you have a better defence for your beliefs.

The second motivation is about who we are and who we want to be. Think for a minute about how you see yourself in the world and how you expect to be treated. Chances are you think of yourself as an agent or a subject: that is, someone who actively chooses how you want to live, what you want to do, and who expects to be allowed to make personal decisions. This is a much better self-conception than, say, a person who is merely a passive object of manipulation or a means to another's end. But if your political decisions are the result of unreflective habit or non-conscious bias, and especially if that habit or bias is due to manipulation by a group or individual, you become less an agent or a subject and more an object.

This risk of being an object instead of an agent/subject leads back to why making good political decisions is so important and brings us to the third and final motivation: each of us individually and all of us collectively has a right to self-determination. That does not mean that anyone or any group can do whatever they want; after all, we must live together, and that requires rules, compromise, and bargaining. But it does mean that the process by which we decide how to live our personal lives and live together publicly should be based on systems in which each person and group can decide, free from manipulation, what they want for themselves.

If reaching better conclusions, resisting manipulation, or asserting the right to decide for yourself how you want to live and how we should live together doesn't motivate you to want to make good political decisions, then little, if anything, will. But I am betting that one of these—or all three of them—does motivate you. And that is a good start. But once that motivation is secured, it must be renewed time and time again, lest you slip back into autopilot. So open up whatever program you use to play music and stick "Eye of the Tiger" on repeat. Imagine yourself as Rocky

Balboa, jumping rope, running at dawn, gulping down raw eggs, and pumping iron — or imagine yourself doing the political decision-making equivalent of that. As you work to stay motivated, there are some other practices you can pursue to make that motivation count. And one of the most important of those is being open to the emotional side of rationality.

Arational receptivity, or politics as therapy

You can't help but be influenced by your emotions when making a decision about politics — and pretty much everything else, for that matter. Emotions are part of what makes us human after all. We should neither expect that we should nor think that we can do away with them when making political decisions. The fact that we make political choices under some emotional influence isn't why we make bad ones. We make them because we rely too much on our emotions, or we make decisions based on factors that we can't account for, even some that we may be unaware of. One of the tricks to making better political decisions, then, is being aware of all the factors that go into a decision, including emotions, hence my tongue-in-cheek reference to "politics as therapy." After all, "Know thyself" has been good advice for millennia.

But what does it mean to be aware of your emotions or, to use some scholarly jargon, open to arational receptivity? When something is "arational," it is *not rational*. It's outside of the scope of rationality. That doesn't mean it's *irrational*, however, which means something nonsensical or illogical. So being open to arational cues means that you must make a conscious effort to isolate, question, and understand the emotional commitments or entanglements that contribute to your values, interests, preferences, and decisions. This is tough to do, especially since a lot of emotional work happens non-consciously. You must dig deep, and there is no guarantee that you will ever recognize all the attachments you have.

So how does this work? Step one is abandoning the rationalist ideal of "the econ." This is what we call the mythical, wholly rational, calculative, and solitary human who is only out to find the most efficient means to their desired ends—the one that is used and abused by social scientists as a tool for modelling or an ideal to aspire to. In its place, you should think of people as rational but bounded in their rationality, emotional, and shaped and constrained by their community. This is not a new approach. Lots of thinkers have made the point that emotion does a lot of necessary work in our thinking. The neuroscientist Antonio Damasio, whose books include *Descartes' Error, Looking for Spinoza*, and *The Feeling of What Happens*, has explored how reason and emotion intermingle in human thought. The more that we understand that we are influenced by rational, emotional, and mixed-thought modes, the more of our processes we can comprehend when it comes time to make a political decision. This approach, rather than compromising rationality and autonomy, enhances both.

This approach is also consistent with what psychologists are learning about humans as "creative thinkers."[7] As psychologist David Pizarro and his colleagues put it:

> Mounting evidence suggests that an exclusively reason-
> based view of moral judgment is wrong as a psychological
> theory. Not because people do not reason at all when they
> make moral judgments...but because other processes are
> at work as well. There is evidence that everyday moral
> judgment is a much less rigid, more emotional, and more
> flexible process than previously described.[8]

So when it comes to reasoning about moral (and other) issues in politics, we have some work to do if we want to make better political decisions, but that work must be consistent with and honest about who we are as humans.

Step two is being open to recognizing and admitting justifications that have emotional content—something along the lines, for instance, of "I like this," "It feels right," or, on the contrary, as in the example offered by Haidt, "This disgusts me."[9] Researchers have demonstrated the coherent, important information in emotional content such as disgust.[10] Simply try-ing to ignore emotion or pretend that emotional responses are irrelevant, accidental, or even undesirable is counterproductive. But the recognition of an emotional attachment or a revulsion should be treated as a *starting point* in the process of making a political decision. If, upon reflection and interrogation, you find that you can't come up with more public rea-sons — that is, exterior reasoning that is understandable to all — that is fine. You have learned something about your decision-making process and you can move on. At the very least you will have ended up with a more autonomous and rational understanding of the matter at hand, even if that merely includes the awareness that an emotional disposition drives you.

Consider, for instance, a debate over polygamy — the practice of having multiple spouses. Since most governments regulate marriage, this is a political issue. Most jurisdictions outlaw polygamy, though the practice has been defended on the grounds of tradition and religion. Some have gone so far as to suggest that it is a matter of personal liberty: if consenting adults freely agree to enter a polygamous arrangement, why permit the state to stop them? Now, take a moment to consider your position on polygamy. Should adults be allowed to marry more than one person if everyone in the arrangement is aware of what's going on and consents to it? A common reaction is to assert that the practice is simply *wrong* or even *disgusting*. But neither of these conclusions is what I would call a good one in the sense of being rational or autonomous — not unless you do a bit more work. And if we move the matter from these pages into the public sphere where we must make decisions about what we should do about polygamy, then we need reasons that are more public — accessible to those taking part in the decision-making process — than asserting that the practice is wrong or disgusting.

Upon reflection, you might discover that your opposition to the practice is rooted in the idea that it's merely different than what you are used to. In that case, your opposition to polygamy is merely the product of prejudice. But once you start to explore your feelings, you might discover that your opposition is linked to how the practice tends to work:

males wedding (often younger) females and often engaging in exploitive techniques that, in fact, undermine the freedom of some of those who "consent" to take part in the arrangement. Your disgust might thus be linked to concerns about the practice being sexist and abusive—even predatory—and a violation of your underlying beliefs that human beings ought not to be exploited. Or perhaps your emotional disposition toward the matter is not *really* about these concerns, but using your feelings as a jumping-off point leads you to the arguments you find persuasive. Either way, engaging with your emotions has helped you reach a more rational, autonomous conclusion.

Being open to engaging with arational influences on your thinking can help lead you to a greater awareness of why you believe the things you do. That process may transform your beliefs or it may reaffirm them. It may not always work, but you will become aware of a blind spot in your thinking. Perhaps, you will become a bit humbler about your position and open to revisiting it in the future. But either way, unless you acknowledge and try to understand how arational influences affect your thinking and decision-making, you will have a much harder time making better political decisions.

Cognitive diversity, or decision-making as a potluck dinner

Political decision-making is a community affair. Not only are political decisions often made by and for groups, but the process of making a decision, even when you are alone, involves many people. It is hard to think outside the time and place in which you exist, and it's impossible to transcend all the commitments you have or the influences of your past. After all, these things contribute to who you are. Thinking and decision-making is always contextual and temporally bound—caught up in the spirit of the time in which they take place. That said, political decision-making can involve more diversity or less (think of which sort of news sources you consult, for instance, and ask yourself whether they represent one viewpoint or if they are ideologically diverse).

In his book *Pluralism*, political theorist William E. Connolly writes—now, bear with me for a moment—"A majority assemblage in a culture of multidimensional pluralism is more analogous to a potluck supper than a formal dinner." He means that in a society in which many people disagree with one another, bring different traditions and commitments to the table, and wish to live in various sorts of sometimes incompatible ways, a commitment to diversity means that getting to majority agreement requires all kinds of different folks doing different kinds of work in different kinds of places. Or, as Connolly puts it, "through a series of resonances between local meetings, internet campaigns, television exposés, church organizations, film portrayals, celebrity testimonials, labor rank-and-file education, and electoral campaigns by charismatic leaders." Politics, for Connolly, is more than legislatures and elections, and for a democracy to be just and inclusive, it requires a diversity of approaches and groups to get the job done.[11]

Good political decision-making requires diversity, too. I think about the process of coming to conclusions in a way that draws on Connolly's conception of pluralism—especially the potluck part. I think that not only does good political decision-making require a diversity of empowered people from a variety of, among others, racial, cultural, class, religious, gender, sexual, and ideological identities, approaches, and backgrounds, but it also requires *cognitive diversity*. Recall that one of the enemies to good political decision-making is cognitive autopilot; it is easy and familiar to rely on your gut, habit, or off-the-shelf shortcuts to reach a decision, but it tends to produce outcomes that are biased, irrational, nowhere near autonomous, and sometimes even unreasonably inflexible.

One way to flip off the autopilot switch is to occasionally engage with a cognitively diverse group that thinks differently and approaches political decision-making in ways that may be unfamiliar to you. Political scientist Hélène Landemore defines cognitive diversity as "a diversity of ways of seeing the world, interpreting problems in it, and working out solutions to these problems," specifically diverse "perspectives," "interpretations," "heuristics," and "predictive models."[12] Having a diverse set of people who think differently, whether you consult them in person or read a variety of news sources, may give you the cognitive jolt you need to think differently. It can nudge you out of your comfort zone, upset your habits, and encourage you to think more rationally and autonomously.

Experience from the business world suggests that cognitive diversity is a valuable tool in decision-making contexts in which conflict might arise. Having people in a room working through what researchers characterize as "disagreements about the issues such as appropriate choices of alternative policies or differences of judgment about the decision" produces better outcomes.[13] It may even help mediate disagreements among management executives (who are not typically conflict-shy people). Cognitive diversity encourages people to turn off the cognitive autopilot that steers them towards bias, and it can also produce better decisions by bringing a variety of perspectives to the table.

Of course, there will always be some folks who are convinced they have it all figured out; they are sure that no one who thinks differently from them has anything to offer when it comes to thinking through political issues. For those people, cognitive diversity might seem a bit pie-in-the-sky. But they are mistaken. To come up with more rational, autonomous political decisions, sometimes you need to move outside your comfort zone and engage with people who think differently from you. As tough as that might be, you will be better off for having committed to it.

Preparedness, or knowing where the potholes are

"If you can dream it, you can do it!" is terrible advice. Or, to be a bit more generous, it is unhelpful and incomplete. The trick to getting things done well is not dreaming—at least not on its own. Success takes planning and effort turning those plans into concrete, actionable tasks. Cognitive bias is everywhere, but a lot of it can be mitigated and managed, if you are prepared to try. Let's look at some specific ways you can address cognitive biases and other challenges to good political decision-making, starting with framing effects.

In chapter four I talked about how framing and other media effects could distort information while shaping how you think about an issue. Framing effects are common, but they are not infinitely powerful. Like most cognitive biases, they are bossy and pushy but not totalitarian. With framing, as political scientist James Druckman puts it, "the effects predictably occur, but only under very specific conditions." He lists several countervailing forces that undermine or eliminate framing effects, including "high personal involvement in the issue" (caring matters), "briefly think[ing] about his or her decision" (even choosing to *briefly* exercise your capacity for rationality and autonomy helps), or having "high cognitive ability" (it never hurts to be smart and, of course, to know what to watch out for).[14]

In a similar vein, philosopher Daniel Dennett, in his essential work *Intuition Pumps and Other Tools for Thinking*, lists dozens of tools for better thinking.[15] Two of them stand out for our purposes. The first is *make mistakes*—but *good mistakes*. And, more to the point, *learn from them* (or, even better, learn from the mistakes of others). The general idea here is that you need to accept that mistakes are not only natural and unavoidable, they are also useful for learning, adapting, and improving future performance. No professional basketball player sinks every basket. No musician hits every note. No person can avoid ever getting tripped up with a tricky decision, fooled by some political snake-oil salesperson, or even misled by their own bias. The trick here is to embrace the writer Samuel Beckett's dictum: "Ever tried. Ever failed. No matter. Try again. Fail again. Fail better." It's fine to make mistakes. That's going to happen. The key to doing better is to learn from them, to move on—instead of digging in and rationalizing them—and to improve going forward.

The second useful piece of advice Dennett offers is to *beware of and avoid deepity*. This is especially good advice for politics. Deepity is "a proposition that *seems* both important and true—and profound—but that achieves this effect by being ambiguous." He gives the example "Love is just a word." What does that mean? Your guess is as good as mine. Politics is full of deepities, often in the form of sloganeering (see if you can identify whose campaign slogans these are): "Make America great again," and "The land is strong." Political speeches are routinely punctuated by deepities, taking forms such as, "Our resource is our people," "United, we can't fail," "I believe in a free country." The key here is *ambiguity*. Beware attempts by politicians and their strategists to let you fill in the blanks or imagine what they might mean by a slogan or sentence. This encourages you to project some wishful thinking onto the blank canvas of their speech.

Iteration, or practice makes perfect

By this point, you have realized that good political decisions do not come naturally to anybody. In fact, while we might think of ourselves as political animals, as Aristotle put it, this refers to our drive to live together in communities, not our inherent capacity to make rational, autonomous decisions once we have assembled. In fact, because many of our impulses challenge our ability to reflect critically on our decisions and what motivates us to make them, good political decision-making requires learning to override what comes easiest to us: going with our gut or taking shortcuts. Because of that, good political decision-making takes *practice*, or repeated tries—what is known as iteration.

There are two reasons why iteration is important for good political decision-making. First, practice makes perfect. Making good political decisions requires you to exercise specific skills in specific ways, some of which aren't likely to come naturally. So you need to train yourself, and that requires regular practice. One of the funny things about contemporary liberal democracy is that while we expect people to have political opinions, and we think that it's a good thing that they do—otherwise how are you, as a citizen, going to get what you want from your government?—we rarely ask people to do more than obey the law, pay taxes, serve on a jury if asked, and vote. So our citizenship expectations are at the same time too low (we do not ask much of people) and too high (because people do not regularly practise good political decision-making, it is hard for us to get right). But when citizens do get the chance to take democracy into their hands under favourable conditions — with time, motivation, and resources — they do a good job.

And that is why it is important for us to get the conditions right for good political decision-making. Earlier, I mentioned the concept of biased pluralism — the notion that some groups have more power and influence that tend to last through generations, creating an "in" class and an "out" class of citizens or residents. One of the reasons biased pluralism persists is that resources are not equally distributed throughout the population, including resources needed for political participation — and regular political decision-making practice.

In the 1990s, political scientists Henry E. Brady, Sidney Verba, and Kay Lehman Schlozman developed a "resource model of political participation."[16] They studied how — and which — Americans participated in the political process and found that the key participatory resources were "time, money, and civic skills — those communications and organizational capacities that are essential to political activity." It is obvious how money acts as a barrier to political participation. It is hard to participate if you can only meet the basic needs of food, shelter, and other daily family commitments — and harder still if you can't. It takes more than subsistence to be able to take part in politics. And some groups have access to more money than others that gives them a leg up.

But what about civic skills? Everyone has these, right? Brady and his colleagues found that civic skills, while acquired at home and in school when people are young, are developed further in adulthood through practice in all sorts of nonpolitical spaces, such as religious institutions, civic organizations, voluntary associations, and at work. These skills tend to favour the well-off, who have more money and often more leisure time, giving them the chance to further develop and practise those skills. People with more education are also likely to have these skills and more chances to practise them.

The second reason iteration is so important is that repeated political decision-making efforts will help wash out *some* of the randomness of some of our choices. Rationality and autonomy are tricky capacities. There will always be days on which we reach conclusions that we wouldn't under different circumstances. Maybe you are having a bad day: you missed the bus and were late, you got into an argument with your partner, you were up late the night before with your friends, and you are, well, you are not feeling your best this morning — life happens. Maybe you are hungry — or, worse, hangry. Or maybe you have yet to come across the information or arguments to help you to a breakthrough on a decision. These same issues are equally applicable to a group. Different factors can contribute to decisions that a group makes so even when you assemble people to reach a decision, randomness may still play a determining part in what sort of choice is made.

From the perspective of making good political decisions, randomness is bad news. Good political decisions are based on reasons. They're something we do on purpose. Randomness just happens as it happens, and it goes against the slow, careful, deliberative thought we expect from ourselves and need in order to have productive discussions and debates — the kind that lead to rational and autonomous outcomes. Through process repetition, or practice, we individually and collectively make it more likely that randomness will wash out and we will get a stable outcome. That does not mean that you will never be affected by randomness, but it will help make the effects less likely to influence decisions in the long run.

Let's take an example of a group brought together to deliberate about social assistance. Imagine that the government assembles the group to meet over several weekends. Participants are there to learn about the issue and to discuss reasons for and against a variety of proposals for reforming policies aimed at making sure no one falls through the cracks. No one in the group is an expert — though they have access to experts, who are tasked with educating the group as the members see fit. (This is a real thing that happens. It is called a citizens' assembly, and I will have more to say about it in the next chapter.) What happens if a few participants are deeply anti-welfare and wildly charismatic? They speak well, with confidence and authority, even though they may not be in possession of all the facts. Before long, they have convinced enough people that the more generous benefits are, the less likely people are to work, so *any* increase in rates is a bad idea. Never mind that this is a bad policy justification because they have not been able to back their arguments up with facts. The people at the table have been caught up by the arguments of the charismatic few. This is not an instance of good political decision-making, since rationality and autonomy have been compromised by a sloppy use of heuristics and something known as affective contagion — transferring emotional content throughout a group.[17]

But what if, over time, as the group meets, they break into smaller groups, shuffling who is in which group from time to time, separating the charismatic few? And what if there were a few different groups established across the province? Over time, as these meetings are repeated and participants avail themselves of some of the practices I have mentioned above, you'll find randomness more likely to get washed out. This is especially true if a lot of the stuff that was driving the bad decision-making was weak. The effects disappeared quickly once they were countered.

Making good political decisions starts with *wanting to make good political decisions*. That may seem self-evident, but in practice it is not. If "good" decisions mean more rational and autonomous decisions — ones that reflect an accurate survey of the facts and an honest understanding of who you are and what you want — then making better decisions requires a commitment to deliberate, sometimes difficult work. This may at times lead you to intellectual and emotional places you would rather not go. After all, who wants to learn that some of their deeply held preferences are motivated by prejudice? Or that their longstanding understanding of some issue has been torqued and distorted by some self-interested third party? You may decide that comfortable and close enough for jazz works for you, thank you very much, and that making better political decisions isn't worth it. But you might also decide, with Socrates, that the unexamined life is not worth living, that to be free means to be aware, whatever that awareness might bring. This requires that you choose to be less an object of someone else's interests and more a self-governing agent.

If you decide on the freedom route, you will need to develop or improve certain intellectual and emotional skill sets, broaden the sorts and range of information sources you consult, and amend how you think about thinking. You will have to increase how often you are willing to do a deep dive into your own motivations, be willing to have political discussions and debates more regularly, and increase your willingness to engage with a diversity of people and their perspectives. Above all, you will need to choose to be as aware and honest as you can be about what underlies the political decisions you make. This is a more difficult way of being in the world than operating on cognitive autopilot, especially when you are just starting out on the road to better political decision-making. But it is a small price to pay to be more autonomous, free, and able to assert your right to decide for yourself what sort of world you want to live in.

9. You cannot fix it all on your own:
Why our milieu and institutions must change

It takes personal effort to make better political decisions. But individuals cannot and should not be expected to do the work of making rational, autonomous political decisions on their own. Making good decisions requires institutional support to encourage those decisions and to translate them into outcomes that inspire people to keep making them. This means that leaders must be responsive to citizens, and that requires building regular, inclusive, and meaningful participatory democratic mechanisms into communities and all levels of government. To achieve this, we need to adapt our milieu and our institutions to facilitate more citizen-led leadership. Even modest changes would be a good start: they would empower citizens to press for more change in the future.

Without these changes, citizen participation in self-government will be at risk of becoming (or remaining) a mere act of "democracy washing"—a tool for politicians to convince one another and the public that they care about citizen engagement when they are merely interested in making it *seem like* they care about public input. To make these changes happen, we need to shift how we think about citizen participation and politics. We need a reset to make sure there is space for people to take part in individual and collective self-determination. This will give us a chance to build a better pluralist society by facilitating fair distribution of power so that no one group can dominate to the detriment of others. And we had better get started right away.

...

I am a utopian in the morning, but by the evening, I moderate my expectations. It is a daily seesaw for me. My utopian mornings are useful, since they provide an ideal through which I can develop, and against which I can measure, realistic reforms. Indeed, utopian thinking—or, perhaps, "regulative ideal" thinking—is useful as a guide and a tool of inspiration. It serves as a reminder that big problems beg for big solutions. After all, marginal tinkering is often not only insufficient for dealing with intractable problems but may even preserve those problems, baking them into the status quo.

Conversely, accepting the status quo as natural, inevitable, or acceptable is an admission of defeat—it's the defeat of politics and of justice. Politics didn't end in the 1950s after the Second World War, the era often labelled the end of ideology, nor did it end in the 1990s after the fall of the Soviet Union, prematurely dubbed the end of history. And universal justice was not achieved with the expansion of liberal democracy. Liberal democracy is neither inevitable nor irreversible. Moreover, it is subject to blind spots and structural injustices that suppress those who find themselves marginalized, exploited, or forgotten and are striving to get what they deserve. We can do better. And that starts with better political decision-making.

A strong environment that protects democracy through better citizen decision-making needs at least four key features: slowness, abundance of time, deep diversity, and equality. Each of these is valuable on its own, but together they form a powerful assemblage that could transform not only how we do politics but how we live.

Slowness

We often celebrate speed. Look how quickly you can send a message from one part of the globe to the other. Imagine how fast the Hyperloop would get you from Vancouver to Los Angeles. Remember Concorde and supersonic trips from New York to London? Bullet trains. Online transactions that take minutes—or seconds!—to complete. Deliveries that take just a day to arrive. Music, television, and film accessible immediately, at any time of day or night. Emails returned within moments of being sent. We praise speed because it enables us to get what we want the moment we want it and allows us to get more done. We rarely stop to consider the implications of that speed, whether the *now* and *more* have made our lives better and us happier.

There is a place for speed in our lives, plainly. But we ought to question when and where it's appropriate, and to what end. In the political realm, if speed creates pressure to respond to more questions faster, then we might decide that the effect of that pressure—for example, further marginalizing citizens who can't keep up with the pace—is not good.

Think of what speed in politics does to politicians. It encourages quick solutions and quick responses, regardless of whether or not they are adequate or substantive. Speed encourages things like omnibus bills in parliament and shortened debate so that elected officials can swiftly move on to the next thing. It encourages governments to turn increasingly to technocrats, the "experts," to do the job, because their expertise allows them to get it done in a timely manner and takes it off the elected official's plate.

For citizens, speedy politics means that they are expected to have opinions and preferences about public matters that they have had little time to reflect on. In an era in which news cycles are packed with quickly evolving stories, and in which social media news may be fast but manipulated or untrue, speed drowns people in a rushing deluge of information. Moreover, social media also allows users to respond to this flood of news and commentary in real time, pressuring them to do it *right away* and to indulge in "just one more click." We get more decisions of lower quality, since time to think is constrained as speed picks up.

As citizen speed demons, people must make up their minds about what they think about a policy or how they intend to vote, but there is not enough time to think properly, so the allure of heuristics as quick, handy tools for deciding is practically irresistible. But, as I hope I have convinced you by now, that is rarely a winning strategy if your goal is to make *good* political decisions and not just good-enough-sometimes political decisions. Slowing down politics means moderating the pace at which information flows—or, at least, is consumed—and extending the time citizens have to address the issues of the day.

Now obviously the toothpaste is out of the tube and onto the counter and floor when it comes to how fast the world moves—for now. It is unlikely that the pace of business media, social media, and law- and policy-making is going to slow down significantly. But we might get some guidance from the *ideal* of slowness that we can apply to *specific* issues and *specific* ways of consuming media. Imagine that the Canadian government has decided to reopen the constitution to address a longstanding political controversy: the Senate. You may like the Senate as it is. You might like the Senate as it was a decade or a century ago. You might want to abolish it. You might want senators to be elected. You might want to turn the Red Chamber into a daycare or a paintball arena. You might not care. But the matter itself is politically significant.

This is a great issue to hive off from the frenetic pace of daily politics and over which to hold deliberations, town hall assemblies, constituency meetings, travelling parliamentary committees, and all kinds of participatory engagements over the course of a year or more, providing a slow drip of information and news coverage as you go. Media organizations could devote special sections to the matter, slowly assembling a comprehensive trove of resources over time for citizens to consult.

It is not that this doesn't happen. From the Berger Commission in the 1980s that changed how we dealt with the Arctic regions to the Truth and Reconciliation hearings on residential schools more recently, these meetings and consultations have been transformative in our understanding of our nation, and they have changed political policy, but they often fail to go far enough or to be as welcoming of and responsive to citizen input as they must. And they're rarely as deliberative—based on reason giving more than political strategizing—as they should be.

A good example of such failure is the national debate over electoral reform in Canada in 2015 and 2016. It went nowhere, even though the Liberal Party promised to do away with the country's electoral system and replace it with some alternative. After months of half-hearted consultation by town hall and half-baked consultation through a confusing website, the Liberal government broke its promise with some vague hand waving about a lack of consensus and concerns about how a different system would encourage the rise of extremist parties. No deliberation. No deep, national policy dive. Just a mess.

More chances at meaningful, deliberative citizen engagement would be welcome, including for issues that are more pressing and time constrained, such as the budget, tax policy, or foreign aid. Indeed, they are necessary to save democracy. But they must be held in ways that put citizens first, give them the resources they need to participate in a meaningful way, and then take their input seriously. The trick is to start early, to commit to a robust process, and to set a timeline and stick to it so that everyone can manage their time. While you can't take this approach for every issue, you can take it for some, creating islands of tranquility in the roaring sea.

Abundance of time

Time is related to speed, but it is not the same thing. You might think that getting things done faster means you have more time to do other things — and logically, that could be true. But if you use that time to move on to the next thing at breakneck speed? Then although you *have time* you are not *taking your time.* When I call for a milieu in which people have an abundance of time, I think of a space in which citizens have adequate, protected time to focus on making good political decisions at a pace conducive to getting the job done well.

A call for more time might seem obvious — and innocent — enough, but it is damn-near a call for revolution. In contemporary liberal democratic societies, we tend to privilege individual, private pursuits over public pursuits. We tend to be good at raising our families and going to work but less good at taking part in collective self-government, in making public decisions about how we wish to live together. We emphasize the "liberal" bit—individualist, private, market-focused—of "liberal democracy" over the "democracy" bit—participation in deciding how to live together.

Making time for good political decision-making means accommodating the time needed to take part in public self-determination. This means that we need to slow down at least *some* of our politics. We need to create and protect time for reflection and deliberation within a *system* that allows individuals to have a bit more time *to specifically think about politics*. People need to have time to access and reflect upon daily news, government documents, political party information, and, critically, to talk to other people who are thinking about politics—whether they are friends, family, colleagues, activists, politicians, journalists, experts, or others.

The word *system* is important here, as are the words *regular basis*. As I mentioned earlier, practice is essential to making better political decisions in the same way that practice is necessary to improve at playing a musical instrument or excelling at a sport. People need time to learn and think about political issues *every day*, even if it is just thirty minutes. They also need the time to take part in participatory politics—town halls, meetings with their elected representative, public deliberations, budgeting exercises, and so on. Modest daily learning and reflection, combined with the occasional town hall and one or two larger public commitments every year or two, will add up quickly as the gains from each compound.

But none of this is possible unless people can set aside the time to take part. And for many, that requires the *opportunity*, which is not just the existence of a meeting or public deliberation, but access to sufficient *resources* to be able to make the time and take advantage of chances to participate when they arise.

How might that work? More resource equality would be a start, as I'll discuss in the next section. But there are other ways to help bring people into political decision-making and give them a chance to develop skills and produce good decisions. One way would be to create regular citizens' assemblies for which people would be compensated and given guaranteed, protected time off work, like we do now for jury duty (more on that in a moment). If you think that trial by a jury of your peers is important, why not extend that logic to good political decision-making by a group of your peers? And why not make election day a national holiday — or, better yet, make it a weekend and give people the Friday before off so that they have a few extra minutes to think about who they are going to vote for and to discuss their thinking with their friends or family? Mandatory voting (used in a few dozen countries, including Australia, Belgium, Brazil, Greece, and Mexico) would help, too, since it would get people to the voting booth — and, in the process, force political parties to pay attention to those folks.

With regular opportunities to take part in self-government, with some extra protected time to do so, with sufficient resources to do so, and with — and this is very important — a motivation to do so because government listens to what the people have to say (which they should), folks would not only be able to carve out a bit of room in their lives to make good political decisions, but they'd also be motivated to do so.

Equality

Making good political decisions requires resources of two kinds: fundamental and incidental. Fundamental resources include core skills and tools such as reading, writing, personal communication, critical thinking, civic and media literacy, a working knowledge of domestic and world history, the basics of debate and rhetoric, people with whom you can discuss politics (including experts and elected officials), and ready access to information, both online and offline. Incidental resources include the things we need to make our fundamental resources count: money, time off work to participate, transportation to and from events, and childcare.

To the extent that resources are unequally shared in a society, it is likely that good political decision-making will also be unequal, which affects the outcomes those decisions bring about. In 2014, political scientists Martin Gilens and Benjamin Page published a study of political inequality in the

United States that garnered a lot of attention and even landed the two of them on *The Daily Show*. In "Testing Theories of American Politics: Elites, Interest Groups, and Average Citizens," the two researchers looked at 1,779 policy issues between 1981 and 2002 in which the nation was surveyed about a policy. They found that economic and political elites have significant influence over policy and law in America, whereas, as they write, "average citizens and mass-based interest groups have little or no independent influence."[1] There is a huge gap, as Gilens and Page find, between what non-elites and elites want from government, especially regarding issues such as taxes, social security, the deficit, and other issues central to political life. But those on one side of that chasm are far better serviced than those on the other. In short: money matters: the rich and powerful tend to get what they want while those with less do not, and things are getting worse. Indeed, in America, the majority *does not* rule and it does not look like they will any time soon.

If we are concerned about rational and autonomous political decisions — forgetting for a moment the roles that power and influence play in legislative and policy outcomes — then even basic levels of political and economic equality go a long way. You can see how what might seem like an anodyne statement — when it comes to political decision-making, people should be treated equally — becomes much more complicated once you extend the concept of equality. This kind of equality moves beyond the notion of equality of opportunity (that is, the idea that everyone has a similar chance to try), and pushes it to a point that guarantees that the playing field has been levelled, by ensuring that one's "chance to try" is functionally meaningful.

Taking a more robust approach to equality makes sense if you believe that each person ought to have the right to decide how they wish to live and to live with others. It makes even more sense if you agree that biased pluralism — the idea that in a society some groups enjoy advantages over others that make it hard for disadvantaged individuals and groups to advocate for themselves — is bad for good political decision-making, since it leads to some being structurally marginalized and kept out of the decision-making loop through little or no fault of their own.

Good political decision-making requires some *basic* equality of money, time, knowledge, access to information, and skills. But it also requires another kind of equality, one just as important as the other resources we have been talking about: moral equality. In political decision-making, moral equality means that each individual or assembled group accepts that everyone affected by a political decision has equal moral standing, that their preferences are legitimate, that they deserve to be heard, and that, when engaging with them, you owe them *reasons* for your preferences. This is a political premise that accepts that politics must rise above self-interest. It calls for politics in practice to be more than just strategic behaviour, horse trading, or manipulation.

Of course, you can make a rational, autonomous choice about what to think of an issue or whom to vote for without ever considering the moral equality of others who will be affected by your choice. In fact, that decision, if it was indeed the product of rational and autonomous reflection, would fit well within the definition of a good political decision as I have laid it out in this book. But moral equality takes things a bit further. It reinforces the need for resource equality; after all, if everyone is owed equal standing, that standing can only count if they have a genuine chance to exercise it. But it also implies that you should respect the rationality and autonomy of *others* and not just your own. If everyone is morally equal insofar as they are a citizen with legitimate preferences and interests in a political community, then you should support their efforts to make better political decisions. Once a critical mass of people is committed to this, the likelihood that good decisions can be made collectively goes up, as does engagement, trust, and the legitimacy of the decisions that are ultimately reached.

Deep diversity

You will notice that I am starting to ask a bit more of you, the good political decision maker, to complement what I am asking of our institutions. None of this is easy. But there is both a moral and a practical, self-interested reason to commit to doing what it takes to make better political decisions. Morally, our collective life is premised on the idea of the inherent worth and dignity of each life. This implies that we ought to respect each person as an agent capable of and having a right to decide for themselves how they prefer to live. If we accept this, then politics becomes the process by which we work out how we will live together in light of those preferences, given scarce resources, disagreement about which ways of collective life are best, and disputes about how to get the job done. Committing to good political decision-making ties you and those around you to the process of respecting, protecting, and extending rationality and autonomy.

Another important reason for making better political decisions is thus clear: those decisions are more legitimate and likely to build trust. Legitimacy and trust are necessary for stable, peaceful democratic life and for the long-term viability of democratic institutions—and, by implication, democracy itself. In the face of growing challenges, including conventional war, nuclear war, environmental catastrophe, resource scarcities, refugee crises, and economic strain or collapse, it will become increasingly important that we make good political decisions.

A commitment to accepting diversity as a fact of life in contemporary democratic states means also accepting that different ways of seeing and being in the world are here to stay. Large populations will increasingly comprise individuals and groups with different histories, values, perspectives, and preferences, and those features will need to be factored into our political decision-making. Accepting diversity also implies the need to build broad, ad hoc coalitions to address the issues of the day, as Connolly calls us to do in his pluralism-as-potluck-dinner metaphor. Once we do this, we can accept that part of making better political decisions is recognizing our own subjectivity and how it relates to others.

Engaging with diversity doesn't mean giving up your preferences or values or declaring "Well, anything goes!" But it does require you to accept that there are other potentially legitimate—if radically different—ways of doing things and attendant sets of preferences that are up for discussion in the public sphere. In effect, the act of accepting diversity creates more space in the public sphere, which is necessary to, over time, make political decisions that are acceptable to a diverse public. It also opens new perspectives for you personally, which may broaden and enhance your own capacity for rational and autonomous thought. The converse—digging in and protecting prejudice or ignoring different perspectives because they are unfamiliar—abdicates rational and autonomous politics.

Improvements to the world around us aimed at facilitating better political decision-making need to be supported by good personal practices and hospitable institutions if we want to improve the quality of the decisions we make. Think of it this way: in a hockey game, there are three sorts of things you need to ensure a decent contest. First, you need the right place to play: somewhere with decent lighting and ice that you can skate on. Second, you need players with some basic skills: they need to know how to skate, how to shoot and pass, and a couple of them need to know how to catch or block the puck. Third, you need rules and procedures: time limits, agreements about what counts as a penalty and what the punishment for infractions will be, and things to facilitate the game and keep it moving like faceoffs, icing, and limits to how many players can be on the ice at once.

Earlier I discussed institutions as "the rules of the game," a phrase coined by economist Douglass North. Consider again what it means for institutions to be rules—and think about what rules are. Rules are implicit or explicit understandings that determine the boundaries for how something is to be done. They do not typically specify the substantive content of an endeavour, but they do outline its form. Rules can be formal or informal. Keeping with our hockey example, a formal rule is that when the puck goes out of play, a faceoff is held. An informal, and typically observed rule, is that during warm-ups you shouldn't shoot the puck high on the goalie. In Canadian politics, it's a formal rule that for a bill to become law, it must pass both the House of Commons and the Senate and receive royal assent. It is an informal rule that opposing parties should not attack the family members of their colleagues and opponents.

In this section, I am interested in rules broadly conceived as a subclass of the ways political decisions are made. There are in fact very few rules in Canada about how politicians make decisions, beyond some formal requirements for passing legislation and the need for decisions to be within the boundaries of the law. When consulting the public on decisions, there are some informal rules, and a few formal rules about public notices and opportunities for input, but politicians are given a lot of room to do what they wish.

That is fine. We elect representatives to make decisions for us. And if we do not approve of how they do that job, we can elect someone else to do it. But often it is not that simple. There are concerns around minority rights, limited party choice, electoral systems that produce incentives to vote strategically, political dynasties, concentrated power and authority, and other considerations that functionally limit responsiveness and influence.

To counter this, we must think about how we can set up some decision-making rules, formal and informal, that become accepted as *institutions* — established patterns of behaviour that everyone who plays the game of politics is expected to follow. I am not interested in making every person a politician, nor am I interested in replacing elected representatives. What I want to do is establish enough of a culture of participatory democracy in which ordinary people, when they wish, can meaningfully and effectively make good political decisions and exercise their right to influence public decisions that will impact their lives.

This bit of the project requires governments and civic educators and organizers to do their part in motivating citizens to get involved, to help folks understand how and why politics should matter to them — the flip side to the personal motivation I discussed in chapter eight. University of Michigan political scientist Arthur Lupia understands this challenge well. As he puts it: "Trying to give someone a political text, most of the time, particularly if they're under fifty, well, they're almost always accessing it on an electronic device where they are one click away from watching a cat video if the content is not sufficiently connected to a core concern they have or can imagine at the moment." He gets it. And far from being cynical about political education and participation, he views the challenge of a busy population with plenty of options for how to spend time as a competition for attention — and for meaning. He argues that we need to make sure people know why politics is important and relevant to them and their lives, and we need to make politics accessible and compelling, both intellectually and emotionally. Otherwise, those who want to bring more people into the political decision-making realm risk becoming, as he puts it, "somebody else...trying to sell somebody something they don't want."[2]

The key to making a more participatory democracy work is providing regular opportunities built into the structure of our political system, to motivate people to take part, and to make those opportunities meaningful. It is not enough for a politician to consult the people and then do whatever they want, democracy washing their way to looking like they care what people think. There must also be regular uptake of citizen input on issues. This need not apply to all issues all the time, but it must apply to those issues most likely to have a significant impact on people's lives, and citizen input should always be taken seriously. To get to that point, there are a few institutional commitments I think need to be implemented.

Participatory budgeting

Ancient Greece is the go-to example of participatory democracy, in large part because of the democratic innovations of the city states that comprised it. Recall that as revolutionary and inclusive as the Greek experience was, political life in city states such as Athens was still highly exclusionary, with certain segments of the population — women, slaves, and foreigners, for instance — excluded from the political process. Nonetheless, citizens had routine opportunities to influence policy and law in a way that few throughout the world have enjoyed since. One of the most important democratic experiences in ancient Athens, for instance, was participatory budgeting. As part of the assembly, Athenians routinely voted on budget matters, including laws with spending implications. In our own time, in the 1980s, Brazil developed its own participatory budgeting process, which was first used in the city of Porto Alegre before spreading to dozens of other cities around the country and, later, to many more around the world, including Vancouver, Toronto, Seattle, Chicago, New York, Mexico City, Seville, Paris, and London.[3] The Brazilian model allows municipalities to delegate sections of the budget to citizens, who meet to discuss and deliberate, prioritizing how that money will be spent in their communities.

Political scientists Brian Wampler and Mike Touchton studied participatory budgeting in Brazil and found that the projects delegated to citizens in the budgeting process typically ranged from 5 to 15 per cent of total municipal spending.[4] Perhaps that does not seem like much, but Wampler and Touchton find that the spending goes a long way. Over 120 cities in the country used participatory budgeting between 1990 and 2008, and the ones that did saw increases in education and health-care spending, a decrease in infant mortality, and strengthened civic capacity and institutions. This brought about a lasting increase in transparency and a decrease in corruption.

Participatory budgeting is becoming increasingly common. Above, I listed some of the many cities where it has been tested or used at the municipal or provincial/state level, including Canada where, for example, the Toronto Community Housing Corporation first used the process in 2001. But what if we were to scale up the process for *regular use* at the provincial or even the federal level? Imagine a series of regional assemblies that brought together a sampling of citizens to meet over the course of several months. These assemblies could then send delegates to provincial or federal citizen meetings to set priorities in specific budget domains. A process like this was adopted by the state of Rio Grande do Sul in Brazil.[5] Over four years, more than a million people took part in the process, allocating more than 12 per cent of the state's budget. Even a modest program would empower citizens, build civic capacity, help folks practise and develop good political decision-making skills, and, of course, encourage government responsiveness. It would also permit a greater proportion of the population to take part in the participatory budgeting process. As it stands, only a very small number who happen to live in one of the few cities where a participatory program is in place have such an opportunity.

Citizens' assemblies

Budgets are important, but they aren't the only bit of public policy or law that counts when it comes to self-government. Constitutions and constitutional amendments, major government programs such as universal health care or social assistance, controversial laws on moral issues including assisted dying or sex work, and close-to-home policies or plans regarding local development or transit shape people's lives. Building in part from the ancient Greek tradition of participatory democracy, a citizens' assembly is a tool that cities, provinces or states, national governments, and supra-national governing bodies around the world can use to help shape and determine policy and law.

I have discussed the citizens' assembly a few times already in this book because, well, I think it is a great way to make political decisions, and I am excited by it. The idea behind a citizens' assembly is simple: bring people together through random, semi-random, or some other form of designed sampling, equip them with as much information as they need (including access to experts), give them time to deliberate over some preselected issue, and then wait for them to make a recommendation for government representatives or officials, or one that would be put to the people at large to decide on. Citizens' assemblies not only give the people a chance to shape political decisions, they also prove that ordinary people can regularly make good political decisions.

Citizens' assemblies have been used throughout the world to inform or make policy decisions. In fact, Canada was a pioneer of the citizens' assembly model and used them in British Columbia in 2004 and in Ontario in 2006 to come up with recommendations for electoral reform that were put to those provinces in 2005 and 2007 respectively. While both referendums were defeated, the 2005 vote on the single transferable vote electoral system in BC received 58 per cent support, just shy of the 60 per cent threshold set by the government for approval.

In Belgium, an assembly known as the G1000 was launched in response to gridlock in the Belgian political system. In 2010, a post-election parliamentary deadlock left the country without a government for *541 days*. The G1000 was a volunteer initiative funded by private donors, including money raised through crowdfunding. Through a three-phase program, the G1000 developed a policy agenda, held a citizens' summit attended by 704 participants, and then held subsequent smaller meetings to turn selected proposals from the summit into policy recommendations. The Belgian experiment with participatory decision-making showed that a sizeable and effective citizens' assembly could be mobilized during fraught political moments and could make people feel like they were a part of something bigger than themselves.

Participatory budgeting and citizens' assemblies are a few encouraging innovations in participatory democracy, but they're the tip of the iceberg. There are dozens and dozens of other processes and tools out there, too. A few years back, professors Mark Warren from the University of British Columbia and Archon Fung of Harvard University came up with the idea of *Participedia*.[6] The idea behind the project was simple: a free, not-for-profit, open, crowd-sourced database of democratic practices and programs around the world. A *Wikipedia*, but for democracy: a one-stop shop for all the participatory democratic ideas you could dream of.

Today, researchers, practitioners, students, and others contribute to *Participedia*, which is supported by dozens of team members, partner organizations, and project staff. And the site lists hundreds of entries from around the world to inspire and guide politicians and citizens towards participatory democracy. So when it comes to bringing citizens into political decision-making, we cannot use the excuse, "Well, we didn't know what to do!" With tools like *Participedia*, help for making better decisions is a click away.

If we want to make better political decisions, we have work to do *both* from the bottom up and the top down. And we had best get to it. A dangerous current in democratic societies carries two often-competing, absolutist imperatives aimed at different targets. The first is the "Think harder!" group represented by those who advocate a return to the old Enlightenment ideal of rationality and autonomy as an achievable state removed from our emotions. Good ol' René Descartes's dualism lives. This camp reads the Enlightenment point of view well enough, but it misreads how humans make their way through the world—emotionally as well as rationally. It also underappreciates how the structures in which we operate condition our thinking. The other camp is the "Let your emotional flag fly!" group, represented by columnist David Brooks. This group argues that gut feelings and other affective drivers are sufficient for making good political decisions.[7] Each of these camps oversimplifies how human cognition and politics interact and therefore offer incomplete assessments and less effective programs for improving political decision-making.

Two other approaches to political decision-making are also troubling because they put too much faith in the institutions. There is the elitist technocrat model—let the experts decide and, for the love of God, keep the masses away from the levers of power. And then there is the populist "Vox populi, vox dei" crowd who suggest that the people, in their infinite wisdom, cannot be wrong and ought to make as many decisions as possible, in whatever way they prefer to decide.

The truth is that good political decision-making requires careful individual engagement, propitious environmental conditions, and plenty of opportunity for practice and applied efforts. Institutions alone can't get the job done, but neither can individuals. Like it or not, for the foreseeable future, we are going to have complex, diverse societies full of institutions that condition our lives, marked by speed and busyness and distractions and all sorts of things that make good political decision-making difficult. We can — and must — still find a way to make better political decisions. To do so, we must work on ourselves and our institutions and build improvements that will support better ways of thinking, judging, discussing, deliberating, debating, and deciding.

Conclusion

Towards better political decisions – and then what?

Every civilization ultimately collapses or at least undergoes fundamental, often painful and traumatic, changes. Perhaps some Sumerians, Greeks, or Romans thought they had reached the end of history, that they had conquered self-government, that they had found not merely *one way* but *the way* of doing things and could continue as they had in perpetuity. As we know, history eventually reveals the hubris in such presumptions.

In the 1990s, political scientist Francis Fukuyama declared that we were approaching the end of history, that liberal democracy was not just ascendant but was the final form of self-organization. As he put it in the 1989 journal article on which he would base his 1992 book *The End of History*, the end of the Cold War was more than the ushering in of a new era, possibly "the end point of mankind's ideological evolution and the universalization of Western liberal democracy as the final form of human government."[1] The years following this rather stunning hubris—optimism, if we are being generous—has proved him wrong.

No human civilization has ever faced the existential threats we do now. It does not help that they are threats of our own making. We have been down to the felt as a species before, near extinct, in fact, but we have not faced anything on the scale that our globalized, technologically sophisticated society has engendered. In a strange, poetic way, the interdependence of our species is bookended at historical extremes. In the beginning, when we were all huddled together, we needed one another to survive. The same is true once more, eons later, though we are now much greater in number and spread widely across the face of the planet. But our survival is very much a collective affair, dependent on the good faith and cooperation of faces we'll never meet nor have a chance to meet.

We humans found our way from survival to flourishing, though never universally. Today as we face unprecedented threats, we are in a moment where we must consciously decide whether our decisions—our *political decisions*—will be made in the service of the long-term survival of ourselves and other species with whom we share the planet, or whether we will abandon our future and await the crash. Our rigidity and failure to aggressively address, for instance, the threat of climate change indicates that at present we are leaning towards the latter. Whether we survive (and flourish) is a political decision that we must make individually and collectively, since the nature of our future depends on what we choose to accept as individuals and practise as a community.

History is always prepared to teach us if we are willing to listen. Lewis Lapham, the former editor of *Harper's Magazine*, extolled the virtues of education—especially engagement with our past—when he wrote: "Unlike moths and goldfish, human beings deprived of memory tend to become disoriented and easily frightened. Not only do we lose track of our own stories—who we are, where we've been, where we might be going—but our elected representatives forget why sovereign nations go to war. The blessed states of amnesia cannot support either the hope of individual liberty or the practice of democratic self-government."[2] Lapham is correct. Indeed, "the blessed states of amnesia" include not only forgetting why nations go to war but also why states and civilizations falter, fail, and vanish into history.

By *forgetting* I do not necessarily mean *not remembering*. Surely *some* of history's lessons have been quite literally forgotten, but many are still right in front of us, accessible in the stories we tell, the books we read, the programs we watch, the podcasts we download. We know the story of the fall of the Sumerians, the Greeks, the Romans, the Khmer, the Mayans, the Olmecs, and others still. We know the patterns of behaviour that lead to collapse, including internal causes such as widespread inequality and greedy, extractive industries or external causes such as war and invasion. We have a pretty good sense of what we should do and what we should not do, though we cannot always agree on precisely which is which, or how we might pursue the former and shun the latter.

Decisions about how we should live together are also decisions about whether we are going to survive and flourish as states and as a species—or, at the very least, decisions about how we might maximize our odds of doing so. These decisions, to be good, require us to remember history, to think history into the future while drawing on our ever-increasing knowledge about the world and how it and the phenomena inside it work. They also require a decision-making process and an environment in which choices are made that are conducive to producing good decisions and limiting bad ones. We face the risk that once things start to get really bad, rather than rising to the occasion—setting aside our biases, our narrow self-interest, our tribal loyalties—we'll descend deeper into automatic, irrational politics. This descent will only make things worse, initiating a cycle that will hasten collapse.

Let's go back to Sumer, between 2037 and 2004 BCE, in the dying days of the Third Dynasty of Ur and what historian Susan Wise Bauer calls "the first environmental disaster." She takes us to Sumeria's ancient plains where, for hundreds of years, cities "had grown enough wheat to support their burgeoning populations through irrigation." But the Sumerians had unwittingly been destroying the fertility of the soil they relied on by planting every field each season. This practice contributed to the salinization of the earth—a process in which brackish water evaporates but leaves a bit of salty residue behind, making it harder to grow crops such as wheat, which was a Sumerian staple.

Eventually, the Sumerians realized they were in trouble. They were "not so ignorant of basic agriculture that they did not understand the problem," as Bauer puts it. And yet for political reasons (taxes, bureau-cracy, the military) and geographic reasons (there were few other places to farm), the Sumerian leadership chose not to adopt the "weed fallowing" method that was necessary to rehabilitate the land. Weed fallowing would make it possible to grow the crops they needed to survive but would make the land periodically unusable. A cycle of decline followed saliniza-tion—food scarcity, poorer health, declining tax revenue, a military that could not be paid and therefore did not fight, rebellion, invasion, and collapse. And that was it for Sumer.[3]

What fools! Who knowingly collapses their own civilization? What sort of people ignore environmental catastrophe steaming towards them? There is a modern impulse to dismiss the past as quaint, primitive, and inferior, as if those who lived before us were mere servants to our ambitions of perfectibility. When challenges arise such as nuclear proliferation, epidemics, or climate change, many believe that technology will save us or, more generally, that *someone* will "figure this out." Perhaps that is true, but we must first *decide* to pursue solutions and commit to them. And those are political decisions that require a lot more than technocratic guidance and scientific discovery—especially if many of the solutions to, say, climate change require that we change how we live.

Our survival is a choice. Perhaps our flourishing is, too. We live in a time of prosperity (unevenly distributed) and abundance (often squan-dered). We also live in a time of great capacity and knowledge, though we often underuse, misuse, or abuse these hard-earned goods. Committing to making better political decisions through building an environment of practices and institutions that enable and encourage us to do so is increas-ingly necessary to ensure our survival in the long run.

Human progress relies not only on technological advancement, but also on moral and ethical advancement alongside what Aristotle called "practical wisdom"—a deep commitment to and capacity for doing the right thing, in the right way, for the right reasons. These commitments are not set-it-and-forget-it affairs. Each generation must renew and recommit to doing better, to being better, to human rights, to environmental stewardship, to justice, to fairness, to decency. The natural order of social and political life is not progress, it is decay. To avoid that breakdown, we need to be constantly vigilant. To do that, we need to make good political decisions. And to do *that*, we need to decide to try. And to try hard.

Of course, that does not mean that we will all become expert political decision makers right out of the gate, that we will never make a mistake or get tired or frustrated — or even fail from time to time. No, the idea is not to achieve perfection. The idea is to work at being citizens and to improve our political decision-making. The idea is to do *better* for ourselves, for those around us, and for future generations.

Early on in this book I said that I do not — and will not try to — pre-suppose what the *content* of a good political decision is, since we disagree all the time about how we should live together, which policies and laws we should pursue. But that does not mean that my approach and commitment to better political decision-making is not normative. Nor does it mean that I don't presuppose some fundamental values necessary for making collective life work — and last.

I presuppose that *process matters* — that the *way* we do things is often just as important, and sometimes more important, than *what* we do. That is because process sets rules, guides thinking, and affects who is listened to and which messages make it onto the agenda. It determines whether people trust the system and the outcomes it produces. Most importantly, it affects how and whether we can address the most pressing issues of our time. I also presuppose that the environment in which we make political decisions, the institutions under which those decisions are made, and the sorts of habits and personal practices we adopt while making them matter a lot. We can rationally and autonomously question ourselves, others, and critical matters of law and public policy, or we can alternate between talking past one another and shouting at one another while our problems fester and grow bigger and more intractable. Perhaps most ambitiously of all, I presuppose that committing to a process of making better political decisions will help us address present and future challenges that cause anxiety, anger, sadness, suffering, and even death.

In this century, we face the threats of climate change and the disasters that flow from it — such as flooding, drought, extreme storms — as well as the crises those disasters will generate, including famine, potable water shortages, and refugee crises. We also face the violent threats of conventional or nuclear war and terrorism at home and abroad. We live with massive and persistent inequality. And, of course, there are always important debates over moral issues that affect how we live together — who is "in" and who is "out" in our society, and whether we can even keep the whole thing together. On top of all that are the many other more mundane but important issues that I have raised, such as taxation, housing policy, transportation, education, military spending, and even food safety. The truth is that you never know when a good political decision will save the day, or when a bad one will cause immediate and potentially cascading harm. But we do know that, in the long run, the survival of democracy and of the human species depends on making good political decisions. So let's get to it.

Acknowledgements

This is my first book. It started with an unexpected phone call in which a friend and editor asked, "Are you writing a book?" Now, if you're a writer and someone asks you if you're writing a book, the answer must be "Yes" — or better "Oh, very much so, yes!" So that's exactly what I told Karen Pinchin when she called me a few years ago to ask me if I was writing a book. I offer her my first acknowledgement and thank you. Without her, this book wouldn't have been possible.

And, of course, I couldn't have done this without the fine and talented folks at Goose Lane Editions, especially Susanne Alexander and Alan Sheppard. It has been a pleasure to work with them, and they've made a difficult process far easier than I imagined it could be.

My editor, Susan Renouf made this book more readable, more rigorous, more human, and therefore more useful. Her experience and wisdom were invaluable. My copy editor, Jill Ainsley, is a true reader's champion. Her precise attention to detail alongside an eye towards the reading experience is next-level. I extend my sincerest thanks to each of them and add the important disclaimer that any errors or shortcomings in these pages are all mine — and none of you can have any of them!

I owe my agent, Chris Bucci, a great debt of gratitude. He saw something here from the beginning, and his confidence in me and this project were hugely helpful in getting started — and finished. But I never would have met Chris if it weren't for Natalie Brender, who made the connection. I thank her dearly.

The title of this book was inspired by an episode of CBC Radio's *Ideas*, which featured my doctoral work in 2014. I thank CBC, Paul Kennedy, producers Tom Howell and Nicola Luksic, and the entire team there for that life-changing opportunity.

I spent a lot of time on Facebook and Twitter while writing this book (but *not* as a distraction, obviously). During writing, I would pop on to social media from time to time to ask a question from my friends and followers, and they never disappointed. Writing this book was considerably easier than it would have been without them, so thanks to all those on social media who gave me advice or helped with research. There are far, far too many of them to name or even remember. But they're out there, and I'm very thankful for their help and for the reminder that social media communities can be constructive and kind.

I interviewed several people for this book, some of whom I quoted, some of whose written work I used, and others whose ideas got me thinking in useful ways, even though I didn't use material from our chats. I'm so thankful for those who were so generous to take the time to talk to me, especially since I cold-called every one of them out of nowhere: Arthur Lupia, Barry Schwartz, Brendan Nyhan, Joseph Heath, Dan Levitin, Brian Hayden, Felipe Fernandez-Armesto, Paul Cartledge, Robyn Dunbar, Steven Mithen, and Ronald Wright. When I was young, and even more as I got older, I wanted to be a writer and to write books. But it's hard to know how to do that. It's not like there's a test or a job ad you apply to, not in most cases anyway. I took a bit of an unusual path to get here, and so I owe several thanks to the many people who helped me reach the point where I could write a book that folks might want to read. So thanks to those who supported my writing career along the way and gave me a shot, especially: David Watson, Kate Heartfield, Nick Taylor Vaisey, Sue Allen, Adrian Lee, Charlie Gillis, Karen Attiah, Elias Lopez, and Alison Uncles.

I finished a PhD in political science just before I started writing this book, and some of the (unpublished) research I did during my doctoral years went into these pages. Moreover, a lot of thinking and talking and discussing and debating I did during my period at the University of British Columbia formed the basis of this project, and the privilege of much of that time was due to the government of Canada's Tri-Council Vanier Canada Graduate Scholarship, for which I'm grateful. I'm also very keen to thank those who were a part of that: my supervisor, Mark E. Warren, and the members of my research and evaluation/ defence committee: Andrew Owen, Steven Heine, Bruce Baum, and Genevieve Fuji Johnson. I also owe a special thanks to others at UBC who helped me learn and grow, including Maxwell Cameron, Becca Monnerat, Barbara Arneil, and Allan Tupper.

I'm lucky that I have smart friends willing to read my work or listen to me talk about it and make it better. Without them, my book would have been worse, and the days I spent writing it would have been even worse than that! My sincerest thanks and appreciation go out to them: Drew Gough, Justin Alger, Amanda Watson, Pam Hrick, Celeste Cote, Jennifer Allen, Charlotte Prong, Forrest Barnum, Meagan Auger, Bryan Leblanc, and Garth Griffiths. These fine folks either read chapters or the entire book and gave me critically helpful feedback.

With all that said, two people stand out for special acknowledgement: Meghan Sali, who read this book and made it better, supported me during my writing, and put up with me being a bit of a pain in the ass at times. My deep and eternal thanks to her. And the same eternal thanks to Paul Saurette, my master's supervisor and mentor at the University of Ottawa, who for years has recognized potential in me that I never expected I might have, supported me, and who taught me to see the world in a sharper, kinder, and more sensitive way.

I also wish to respectfully acknowledge that I conducted research and wrote this book on the unceded Coast Salish lands of the Musqueam, Squamish, and Tsleil-Waututh Nations, and finished editing and proofing on the unceded territory of the Algonquin Anishinaabeg.

Notes

Preface

1. Antonio Damasio, *Looking for Spinoza: Joy, Sorrow, and the Feeling Brain* (New York: Mariner Books, 2003), 8.

Introduction

1. Many volumes look at human evolution, the rise of civilization, and the birth of political order. For some comprehensive and highly readable accounts, see Yuval Noah Harari, *Sapiens: A Brief History of Humankind* (Toronto: Signal, 2014); Felipe Fernandez-Armesto, *Humankind: A Brief History* (Oxford: Oxford University Press, 2004); Ronald Wright, *A Short History of Progress* (Toronto: Anansi, 2004); and Francis Fukuyama, *The Origins of Political Order* (New York: Farrar, Straus, and Giroux, 2011).

2. George Lakoff, *Don't Think of an Elephant! Know Your Values and Frame the Debate* (New York: Chelsea Green Publishing, 2014).

3. Freedom House, *Freedom in the World 2018: Democracy in Crisis.*

4. Economist Intelligence Unit, *Democracy Index 2017.*

5. Steven Pinker, *The Better Angels of Our Nature: Why Violence Has Declined* (New York: Penguin Books, 2012).

6. Philip J. Landrigan et al., "The *Lancet* Commission on Pollution and Health," *Lancet* 391, no. 10119 (2017), 462-512.

7. Statistics Canada, "Spotlight on Canadians: Results from the General Social Survey 'Public confidence in Canadian institutions,'" 2017. See also: Conference Board of Canada, "Confidence in Parliament," 2013.

1. Public matters, grey matter

1. Ray Kurzweil, *How to Create a Mind: The Secret of Human Thought Revealed* (New York: Penguin, 2012), 104-5.

2. Some comprehensive and highly readable accounts of ancient
    Mesopotamian farming practices and how they relate to civilizational
    decline include Susan Wise Bauer, *History of the Ancient World: The
    Earliest Accounts to the Fall of Rome* (New York: W.W. Norton, 2007);
    Ronald Wright, *A Short History of Progress* (Toronto: Anansi, 2004); Jared
    Diamond, *Collapse: How Societies Choose to Fail or Succeed* (New York:
    Penguin, 2005); and the classic piece by Thorkild Jacobsen and Robert M.
    Adams, "Salt and Silt in Ancient Mesopotamian Agriculture, *Science* 123,
    no. 3334 (1958), 1251-58.

3. Wright, *A Short History of Progress*, 60-61.

4. Gerald Edelman, *Second Nature: Brain Science and Human Knowledge*
    (Oxford: Oxford University Press, 2006), 21-22.

5. Harari, *Sapiens*, 9.

6. See, for instance, Antonio Damasio, *Descartes' Error: Emotion, Reason, and
    the Human Brain* (New York: Penguin, 2005).

7. Drew Westen, *The Political Brain: The Role of Emotion in Deciding the Fate
    of the Nation* (New York: Public Affairs, 2007), 71.

8. Donald Green, Bradley Palmquist, and Eric Schickler, *Partisan Hearts and
    Minds: Political Parties and the Social Identities of Voters* (New Haven: Yale
    University Press, 2004).

9. André Blais et al., "Political Judgments, Perceptions of Facts, and Partisan
    Effects," *Electoral Studies* 29 no. 1 (2010), 1-12. See also Elisabeth Gidengil
    et al., "Back to the Future? Making Sense of the 2004 Canadian Election
    Outside Quebec," *Canadian Journal of Political Science* 39, no. 1 (2006),
    1-25.

10. Michael Gazzaniga, *The Mind's Past* (Oakland, CA: University of
    California Press, 2000), 21.

11. Christopher Chabris and Daniel Simons, *The Invisible Gorilla: How Our
    Intuitions Deceive Us* (New York: Harmony, 2011). And if you're curious
    whether you'd spot the gorilla, you can take the test yourself on the
    authors' website: www.theinvisiblegorilla.com/videos.html.

12. Charles C. Ballew and Alexander Todorov, "Predicting Political Elections
    from Rapid and Unreflective Face Judgments," *Proceedings of the National
    Academy of Sciences* 105, no. 45 (2007), 17948-53.

13. Rick Shenkman, *Political Animals* (New York: Basic Books, 2016), 24-25.

14. Experts disagree on what drove humans to near extinction, but some suggest our population might have dipped as low as two thousand, possibly because of climate change. See Doron M. Behar et al., "The Dawn of Human Matrilineal Diversity," *American Journal of Human Genetics* 82, no. 5 (2008), 1130-40.

15. Joseph Heath, *Enlightenment 2.0: Restoring Sanity to Our Politics, Our Economy, and Our Lives* (Toronto: HarperCollins, 2014), 353.

16. Wright, *Short History of Progress*, 29-30.

17. Peter Watson, *Ideas: A History from Fire to Freud* (London: Phoenix, 2006), 32.

18. Wright, *Short History of Progress*, 30.

19. Marco T. Bastos and Dan Mercea, "The Brexit Botnet and User-Generated Hyperpartisan News," *Social Science Computer Review* (October 2017), http://journals.sagepub.com/doi/full/10.1177/0894439317734157.

20. Warren Kinsella, *Kicking Ass in Canadian Politics* (Toronto: Random House Canada), 39.

2. Deciding in democracies

1. Francis Fukuyama, *The Origins of Political Order* (New York: Farrar, Straus, and Giroux, 2011), 53-55.

2. Fukuyama, *Origins of Political Order*, 52.

3. Steven Mithen, *After the Ice: A Global Human History, 20,000-5,000 BC* (Cambridge, MA: Harvard University Press, 2003), 3.

4. Paul Cartledge, personal interview, 2017.

5. Paul Cartledge, *Democracy: A Life* (Oxford: Oxford University Press, 2016), 248.

6. Susan Wise Bauer, *The History of the Ancient World* (New York: W.W. Norton, 2007), 692-93.

7. Bauer, *History of the Ancient World*, 480.

8. Cartledge, *Democracy*, 255-57.

9. Cartledge, *Democracy*, 257.

10. Daron Acemoglu and James A. Robinson, *Why Nations Fail* (New York: Crown, 2012), 162- 68.

11. Søren Kierkegaard, Journals and Papers. Volume 1, A-E. IV A 164. Intelex Past Masters. http://www.nlx.com/collections/73.

12. Johan Norberg, *Progress: Ten Reasons to Look Forward to the Future* (London: Oneworld Publications, 2016).

13. Pew Research Center, "Globally, Broad Support for Representative and Direct Democracy," 2017.

14. David Runciman, *How Democracy Ends* (New York: Basic Books, 2018), Cass Sunstein, ed., *Can It Happen Here: Authoritarianism in America* (New York: Dey Street Books, 2018), and Steven Levitsky and Daniel Ziblatt, *How Democracies Die* (New York: Crown, 2018). For a Canadian take, see Michael Adams, *Could It Happen Here? Canada in the Age of Trump and Brexit* (Toronto: Simon and Schuster, 2017).

15. Jennifer Welsh, *The Return of History* (Toronto: House of Anansi Press, 2016), jacket copy.

16. Jennifer S. Hunt, "Studying the Effects of Race, Ethnicity, and Culture on Jury Behaviour," in Margaret Bull Kovera, ed. *The Psychology of Juries* (Washington: American Psychological Association, 2017), 83-107.

17. "Prof. Kent Roach on How the Canadian Legal System Fails Indigenous People Like Colten Boushie," February 14, 2018, www.law.utoronto.ca/news/prof-kent-roach-how-canadian-legal-system-fails-indigenous-people-colten-boushie. See also Kent Roach, "Colten Boushie's Family Should Be Upset: Our Jury Selection Procedure is Not Fair," *Globe and Mail*, January 30, 2018.

18. Edelman, *2017 Edelman Trust Barometer: Global Report* (Edelman Research, 2017).

19. World Bank, *World Development Report 2017: Governance and the Law.*

20. "Voter Turnout by Age Group," Elections Canada, http://www.elections.ca/res/rec/part/estim/42ge/42_e.pdf.

21. Paul Kershaw, *Measuring the Age Gap in Canadian Social Spending* (Vancouver: Generation Squeeze, 2015), https://d3n8a8pro7vhmx.cloudfront.net/gensqueeze/pages/4214/attachments/original/1512083781/Measuring_the_Age_Gap_in_Social_Spending_Final_6Feb2015.pdf?1512083781.

3. What is a good political decision?

1. For a good overview of trust, including what it is, how it works, and what it generates, see Eric M. Ulsander, ed., *The Oxford Handbook of Social and Political Trust* (Oxford: Oxford University Press, 2017). A few chapters of that volume stand out. For trust and economic growth, see Christian Bjørnskov, "Social Trust and Economic Growth." For trust and health, see Ichiro Kawachi, "Trust and Population Health." For trust and well-being, see John F. Helliwell, Haifang Huang, and Shun Wang, "New Evidence of Trust and Well-Being." For trust and polarization, see Marc J. Hetherington and Thomas J. Rudolph, "Political Trust and Polarization." And for a good overview of trust and democracy, see Mark E. Warren, "Trust and Democracy."

2. Adam Rogers, "The Science of Why No One Agrees on the Color of This Dress," *Wired*, February 26, 2015, www.wired.com/2015/02/science-one-agrees-color-dress.

3. See *Current Biology* 25, no. 3 (2015) for the papers "The Many Colours of 'the Dress'" (Karl R. Gegenfurtner, Marina Blog, and Matteo Toscani), "Striking Individual Differences in Color Perception Uncovered by 'the Dress' Photograph," (Rosa Lafer-Sousa, Katherine L. Hermann, and Bevil R. Conway), and "Asymmetries in Blue-Yellow Color Perception and in the Color of 'the Dress'" (Alissa D. Winkler, Lothar Spillmann, John S. Werner, and Michael A. Webster).

4. Manfred Kuehn, *Kant: A Biography* (Cambridge: Cambridge University Press, 2002). See also Luke Harding, "Kant's wild years," *Guardian*, February 12, 2014.

5. Paul Sniderman et al., "Reasoning Chains: Causal Models of Policy Reasoning in Mass Publics," *British Journal of Political Science* 16, no. 4 (1986), 405-30.

6. John Christman, "Autonomy and Personal History," *Canadian Journal of Philosophy* 21, no. 1 (1991), 1-24.

7. Christman, "Autonomy and Personal History," 1.

8. Jennifer Nedelsky, "Judgment, Diversity, and Relational Autonomy," in *Judgment, Imagination, and Politics*, ed. Ronald Beiner and Jennifer Nedelsky (New York: Rowman and Littlefield, 2001), 111.

9. For more on these examples and others, see, for instance, Daniel Kahneman, *Thinking, Fast and Slow* (Toronto: Doubleday, 2011) and

Richard Thaler, *Misbehaving: The Making of Behavioral Economics* (New York: W.W. Norton, 2016).

10. Anthony Giddens, *The Constitution of Society* (Oakland: University of California Press, 1984), 375.

11. I drew on this example in a paper I co-authored with Mark Warren to illustrate deliberation and the all-affected-interests principle. See "When Is Deliberation Democratic," *Journal of Public Deliberation* 12, no. 2 (2016), 8.

12. Transit Cooperative Research Program, *Research Results Digest* 21 (August 1997), http://onlinepubs.trb.org/onlinepubs/tcrp/tcrp_rrd_21.pdf.

13. This entire section is heavily influenced by Mark Warren's work. I draw on several of his ideas, which can be found in the following highly recommended works: *Democracy and Trust* (Cambridge: Cambridge University Press, 1999); *Democracy and Association* (Princeton, NJ: Princeton University Press, 2001); "A Problem-Based Approach to Democratic Theory," *American Political Science Review* 111, no. 1 (2017); and our co-authored article "When Is Deliberation Democratic?".

4. Our bodies, our minds, mental shortcuts, and the media

1. See, for instance, Antonio Damasio, *Self Comes to Mind: Constructing the Conscious Brain* (New York: Vintage, 2010).

2. Joseph Heath, *Enlightenment 2.0: Restoring Sanity to Our Politics, Our Economy, and Our Lives* (Toronto: HarperCollins, 2014), 64.

3. Kahneman, *Thinking, Fast and Slow*, 20-22, 29, 39-46, and 50-52.

4. Daniel Kahneman and Amos Tversky, "The Framing of Decisions and the Psychology of Choice," *Science* 211, no. 4481 (1981), 458.

5. See, for instance, National Public Radio, "How We Got From Estate Tax to 'Death Tax,'" December 15, 2010, www.npr.org/sections/thetwo-way/2010/12/16/132031116/a-history-of-how-we-got-from-estate-tax-to-death-tax.

6. James N. Druckman, "The Implications of Framing Effects for Citizen Competence," *Political Behavior* 23, no. 3 (2001), 225-56. In addition to Druckman, see Dennis Chong, "How People Think, Reason, and Feel About Rights and Liberties," *American Journal of Political Science* 37 (1993), 867-99.

7. James N. Druckman, "What's It All About? Framing in Political Science" in *Perspectives on Framing*, ed. Gideon Keren (New York: Psychology Press, 2010).

8. Shanto Iyengar, *Media Politics: A Citizen's Guide (Second Edition)* (New York: W.W. Norton, 2011), 247-48.

9. Iyengar, *Media Politics*, 232.

10. Iyengar, *Media Politics*.

11. Alvin Chang, "The stories Fox News covers obsessively—and those it ignores—in charts," *Vox*, May 30, 2018, www.vox.com/2018/5/30/17380096/fox-news-alternate-reality-charts.

12. Jon Keegan, "Blue Feed, Red Feed: See Liberal Facebook and Conservative Facebook, Side by Side," *Wall Street Journal*, May 17, 2016, http://graphics.wsj.com/blue-feed-red-feed/#/executive-order.

13. Shanto Iyengar and Donald Kinder, *News That Matters* (Chicago: Chicago University Press, 2010), 116-18.

14. See, for instance, David Lawler, "Hillary Clinton Blames Loss on FBI's James Comey in Call with Top Donors," *Daily Telegraph*, November 12, 2016, and Gearan's tweet: https://twitter.com/agearan/status/797493875225071616.

15. Nate Silver, "The Comey Letter Probably Cost Clinton The Election," *Fivethirtyeight*, https://fivethirtyeight.com/features/the-comey-letter-probably-cost-clinton-the-election.

16. Kahneman, *Thinking, Fast and Slow*, 98.

17. Arthur Lupia, "Shortcuts Versus Encyclopedias: Information and Voting Behavior in California Insurance Reform Elections," *American Political Science Review*, 88, no. 1 (March 1994), 63-76.

18. Philip Oreopoulous, "Why Do Skilled Immigrants Struggle in the Labor Market? A Field Experiment with Thirteen Thousand Resumes," *American Economic Journal* (November 2011), 148-171.

19. Christopher H. Achen and Larry M. Bartels, *Democracy for Realists: Why Elections Do Not Produce Responsive Government* (Princeton: Princeton University Press, 2016).

20. Geoffrey Evans and Mark Pickup, "Reversing the Causal Arrow: The Political Conditioning of Economic Perceptions in the 2000-2004 U.S. Presidential Election Cycle," *Journal of Politics* 72, no. 4 (2010), 1236-51.

21. See, for instance, chapter 10 in Achen and Bartels, *Democracy for Realists,*
    as well as Milton Lodge and Charles S. Taber, *The Rationalizing Voter*
    (Cambridge: Cambridge University Press, 2013).

5. Our milieu

1. See the National Park Service's short history of long-distance
    communication at www.nps.gov/poex/index.htm.

2. Dan Levitin, *The Organized Mind: Thinking Straight in the Age of
    Information Overload* (Toronto: Penguin, 2015), xiv-xv.

3. See the International Telecommunication Union's numbers on internet use
    at www.itu.int/net/pressoffice/press_releases/2015/17.aspx#.WjKyarbMyDV.

4. Levitin, *Organized Mind*, 6-7.

5. Fermín Moscoso del Prado Martín, "The Thermodynamics of Human
    Reaction Times," *Neurons and Cognition* arXiv: 0908.3170 (q-bio.NC).

6. Barry Schwartz, *The Paradox of Choice: Why More is Less* (New York:
    Harper Perennial, 2005), 5, and personal interview, 2017.

6. Our institutions

1. Daron Acemoglu and James Robinson, *Why Nations Fail: The Origins of
    Power, Prosperity, and Poverty* (New York: Crown, 2012).

2. Arthur T. Denzau and Douglass C. North, "Shared Mental Models:
    Ideologies and Institutions," *Kyklos* 47, no. 1 (1994), 3-31.

3. Jonathan H. Turner, *The Institutional Order: Economy, Kinship, Religion,
    Polity, Law, and Education in Evolutionary and Comparative Perspective*
    (New York: Longman, 1997), 6.

4. Office of the Historian, "US Diplomacy and Yellow Journalism, 1895-
    1898," https://history.state.gov/milestones/1866-1898/yellow-journalism.

5. Andrew Guess, Brendan Nyhan, and Jason Reifler, "Selective Exposure
    to Misinformation: Evidence from the consumption of fake news during
    the 2016 US presidential campaign," January 9, 2018, www.dartmouth.
    edu/~nyhan/fake-news-2016.pdf.

6. James B. Jacobs and Ellen Peters, "Labor Racketeering: The Mafia and the
    Unions," *Crime and Justice* 30 (2003), 229-82.

7. Donald R. Kinder and Nathan P. Kalmoe, *Neither Liberal nor
    Conservative: Ideological Innocence in the American Public* (Chicago:
    University of Chicago Press, 2017).

8. Ezra Klein, "For Elites, Politics is Driven by Ideology. For Voters, It's Not," *Vox* (November 9, 2017), www.vox.com/policy-and-politics/2017/11/9/16614672/ideology-liberal-conservatives.

9. Karl Marx, *Capital: A Critique of Political Economy (Volumes 1-3)* (New York: Penguin, 1992-1993).

7. Five ways of thinking about thinking

1. David Dunning, "Motivated Cognition in Self and Social Thought" in Mario Mikulincer and Phillip R. Shaver, eds. *APA Handbook of Personality and Social Psychology*, vol. 1 (Washington: American Psychological Association, 2015), 778.

2. Milton Lodge and Charles S. Taber, *The Rationalizing Voter* (Cambridge: Cambridge University Press, 2013), 35-36.

3. See Dan Kahan, "Ideology, Motivated Reasoning, and Cognitive Reflection," *Judgment and Decision Making* 8, no. 4 (2013), 407-24, and Thomas J. Leeper and Rune Slothuus, "Political Parties, Motivated Reasoning, and Public Opinion Formation," *Political Psychology* 35, supplement 1 (2014), 141-42.

4. See Richard E. Petty and Duane T. Wegener, "The Elaboration Likelihood Model: Current Status and Controversies," in *Dual Process Theories in Social Psychology*, ed. Shelley Chaiken and Yaacov Trope (New York: Guilford Press, 1999), and Richard E. Petty and John T. Cacioppo, *Communication and Persuasion: Central and Peripheral Routes to Attitude Change* (New York: Springer-Verlag, 1986).

5. Richard E. Petty and Stephen M. Smith, "Elaboration as a Determinant of Attitude Strength: Creating Attitudes that are Persistent, Resistant, and Predictive of Behaviour," in *Attitude Strength: Antecedents and Consequences*, ed. Richard E. Petty and Jon A. Krosnick (New York: Psychology Press, 1995).

6. John Bargh and Tanya Chartrand, "The Unbearable Automaticity of Being," *American Psychologist* 54, no. 7 (1999), 462-79.

7. Charles C. Ballew and Alexander Todorov, "Predicting Political Elections from Rapid and Unreflective Face Judgments," *Proceedings of the National Academy of Sciences* 105, no. 45, 17948-53.

8. Luisa Batalha, Nazar Akrami, and Bo Ekehammar, "Outgroup Favouritism: The Role of Power, Perception, Gender, and Conservatism," *Current Research in Social Psychology* 13, no. 4 (2007), 39-49.

9.   John T. Jost and Mahzarin R. Banaji, "The Role of Stereotyping in System-Justification and the Production of False Consciousness," *British Journal of Social Psychology* 33, no. 1 (1994), 2.

10.   John T. Jost, "A Decade of System Justification Theory: Accumulated Evidence of Conscious and Unconscious Bolstering of the Status Quo," *Political Psychology* 25, no. 6 (2004), 881-919.

11.   John T. Jost et al., "Political Conservatism as Motivated Social Cognition," *Psychological Bulletin* 129, no. 3 (2003), 339-75.

8. I want you! (to make better political decisions)

1.   This point is drawn from a rich body of literature on the public sphere and democratic deliberation. The most important theorist of this, Jürgen Habermas, remains one of its earliest. See his classic works *Between Facts and Norms: Contributions to a Discourse Theory of Law and Democracy*, translated by William Rehg (Boston: Polity Press, 1996), and *The Theory of Communicative Action*, translated by Thomas McCarthy (Boston: Beacon Press, 1984).

2.   Many sources address this concept. Two interesting ones are Archon Fung, "The Principle of Affected Interests: An Interpretation and Defense" in *Representation: Elections and Beyond*, ed. Jack H. Nagel and Rogers M. Smith (Philadelphia: University of Pennsylvania Press, 2013) and Robert Goodin, "Enfranchising all affected interests, and its alternatives," *Philosophy & Public Affairs* 35, no. 1 (2007), 40-68.

3.   E.E. Schattschneider, *The Semisovereign People: A Realist's View of Democracy in America* (Belmont: Wadsworth, 1960).

4.   Haeran Jae and Devon Delvecchio, "Decision Making by Low-Literacy Consumers in the Presence of Point-of-Purchase Information," *Journal of Consumer Affairs* 38, no. 2 (2005), 342-54, and Richard E. Petty, Gary L. Wells, and Timothy C. Brock, "Distraction Can Enhance or Reduce Yielding to Propaganda: Thought Disruptions Versus Effort Justification," *Journal of Personality and Social Psychology* 34, no. 5 (1976), 874-84.

5.   "Money Raised as of Dec. 31," *Washington Post*, www.washingtonpost.com/graphics/politics/2016-election/campaign-finance/.

6.   Shawn Parry-Giles et al., "2016 presidential advertising focused on character attacks," *Conversation*, November 16, 2016, https://theconversation.com/2016-presidential-advertising-focused-on-character-attacks-68642.

7. E. Paul Torrance, "Current Research on the Nature of Creative Talent," *Journal of Counselling Psychology* 6, no. 4 (1959), 309-16.

8. David Pizarro, Brian Detweiler-Bedell, and Paul Bloom, "The Creativity of Everyday Moral Reasoning: Empathy, Disgust, and Moral Persuasion," in *Creativity and Cognitive Development*, ed. James Kaufman and John Baer (Cambridge: Cambridge University Press, 2006), 81-98.

9. Jonathan Haidt, "The Emotional Dog and its Rational Tail: A Social Intuitionist Approach to Moral Judgment," *Psychological Review* 108, no. 4 (2001), 814-34.

10. See, for instance, Damasio, *Descartes' Error*; Jonathan Haidt, "The Emotional Dog and its Rational Tail: A Social Intuitionist Approach to Moral Judgment," 814-34; and Simone Schnall et al., "Disgust as Embodied Moral Judgment," *Personality and Psychology Bulletin* 38, no. 8 (2008), 1096-1109.

11. William E. Connolly, *Pluralism* (Durham: Duke University Press, 2005), 9.

12. Hélène Landemore, *Democratic Reason: Politics, Collective Intelligence, and the Rule of the Many* (Princeton: Princeton University Press, 2013), 207. See also Lu Hong and Scott E. Page, "Groups of Diverse Problem Solvers Can Outperform Groups of High-Ability Problem Solvers," *Proceedings of the National Academy of Sciences* 101, no. 45 (2004), 16385-89.

13. Carsten K.W. de Dreu, "When Too Little or Too Much Hurts: Evidence for a Curvilinear Relationship Between Conflict and Innovation in Teams," *Journal of Management* 32, no. 1 (2006), 931-50.

14. Druckman, "Implications of Framing Effects," 236.

15. Daniel C. Dennett, *Intuition Pumps and Other Tools for Thinking* (New York: W.W. Norton, 2013). If you're keen to learn more, a few other good places to start include Rolf Dobelli, *The Art of Thinking Clearly* (New York: HarperCollins, 2014); Kahneman, *Thinking*; Schwartz, *Paradox of Choice*; Cass Sunstein and Richard Thaler, *Nudge: Improving Decisions About Health, Wealth, and Happiness* (New York: Penguin, 2009); Levitin, *Organized Mind*; Heath, *Enlightenment 2.0*; and Dan Gardner and Philip E. Tetlock, *Superforecasting: The Art and Science of Prediction* (New York: Crown, 2015). But don't be overwhelmed by how many options you have to choose from—which might just make the problem worse. Pick a book or two and choose a few approaches, even just one, that appeal to you. And the next time you need to make a political decision—who to vote for, for

instance, or how you feel about a proposed policy—try applying that tool. But don't forget Dennett (and Beckett's) advice to embrace practice and mistakes as part of your decision-making journey.

16. Henry E. Brady, Sidney Verba, and Kay Lehman Schlozman, "Beyond SES: A Resource Model of Political Participation," *American Political Science Review* 89, no. 2 (1995), 271-94.

17. See, for example, Sigal G. Barsade, "The Ripple Effect: Emotional Contagion and Its Influence on Group Behavior," *Administrative Science Quarterly* 47, no. 4 (2002), 644-75.

9. You cannot fix it all on your own

1. Martin Gilens and Benjamin I. Page, "Testing Theories of American Politics: Elites, Interest Groups, and Average Citizens," *Perspectives on Politics* 12, no. 3 (2014), 564-81.

2. Arthur Lupia, personal interview, 2017.

3. For more on what participatory budgeting is and where it's used, see the Participatory Budgeting Project at www.participatorybudgeting.org.

4. Brian Wampler and Mike Touchton, "Brazil Let Its Citizens Make Decisions About City Budgets. Here's What Happened," *Washington Post*, January 22, 2014.

5. Vanessa Marx and Alfredo Alejandro Gugliano, "Participatory Budget in Brazil: The Case of Rio Grande do Sul State," 22nd World Congress of Political Science, International Political Science Association, 2012, http://paperroom.ipsa.org/papers/paper_18448.pdf.

6. You can visit and/or contribute to *Participedia* at https://participedia.net.

7. See Joseph Heath's discussions of the Brooks school of thought in *Enlightenment 2.0*.

Conclusion

1. Francis Fukuyama, "The End of History?" *National Interest* 16 (Summer 1989), 3-18.

2. Lewis Lapham, "The Gulf of Time," https://www.laphamsquarterly.org/states-war/gulf-time.

3. Bauer, *History of the Ancient World*, 139-40.

Index

David Moscrop is a writer, academic, and political theorist who studies democracy, digital media, and political decision-making. His latest research focuses on how knowledge circulates on the internet and how micro-targeting, Big Data, fake news, bots, and hacking threaten citizen participation in democracies.

A columnist and political commentator, Moscrop is a frequent contributor to *Maclean's* and other print and broadcast media, including the *Washington Post*, the *Globe and Mail*, the *National Post*, and CBC Radio. He has also worked as a consultant for the Broadbent Institute, the University of British Columbia's School of Public Policy and Global Affairs, and MASS LBP on topics such as electoral reform, digital media, and participatory democracy.

Moscrop holds a PhD in political science from the University of British Columbia. He is currently a postdoctoral fellow at the University of Ottawa.